Starting with Poetry

ANN C. COLLEY
FISK UNIVERSITY

JUDITH K. MOORE
CORNELL UNIVERSITY

HARCOURT BRACE JOVANOVICH

NEW YORK   CHICAGO   SAN FRANCISCO   ATLANTA

ISBN: 0-15-583757-5

Library of Congress Catalog Card Number: 72-92268

Printed in the United States of America

DEDICATIONS

For Quince,
Jewel L. Kibble,
and especially for Scott.

For the Barton Hall Community;
for English 12K, Spring, 1971;
for Robert;
and for each other.

CREDITS AND ACKNOWLEDGMENTS

MARGARET ATWOOD. "Dreams of the Animals" and "Game After Supper" are reprinted from PROCEDURES FOR UNDERGROUND by Margaret Atwood, by permission of Atlantic-Little, Brown & Company. Copyright © 1970 by Oxford University Press (Canadian Branch).

W. H. AUDEN. "Miss Gee" and "Who's Who" are Copyright 1940 and renewed 1968 by W. H. Auden. Reprinted from COLLECTED SHORTER POEMS, 1927–1957, by W. H. Auden, by permission of Random House, Inc. and of Faber and Faber Ltd.

COLEMAN BARKS. "Big Toe," Copyright © 1968 by Coleman Barks; "Bruises," Copyright © 1972 by Coleman Barks; "Cavities," Copyright © 1972 by Coleman Barks; and "Goosepimples," Copyright © 1968 by Coleman Barks, are reprinted from THE JUICE by Coleman Barks by permission of Harper & Row Publishers, Inc. "Appendix" is reprinted from QUICKLY AGING HERE: SOME POETS OF THE 1970's edited by Geoff Hewitt, © 1969 by Doubleday & Company, Inc.

ELIZABETH BISHOP. "Manners" and "Sestina" are reprinted with the permission of Farrar, Straus & Giroux, Inc. from THE COMPLETE POEMS of Elizabeth Bishop, Copyright © 1955, 1956, 1969 by Elizabeth Bishop.

D. M. BLACK. "The Educators" is reprinted from THE EDUCATORS by D. M. Black, © 1969 by D. M. Black and published by Barrie & Jenkins Ltd. by permission of Barrie & Jenkins Ltd. and the author.

ROBERT BLY. "Sleet Storm on the Merritt Parkway" from THE LIGHT AROUND THE BODY by Robert Bly. Copyright © 1962 by Robert Bly. Reprinted by permission of Harper & Row Publishers, Inc.

GWENDOLYN BROOKS. "Song in the Front Yard," Copyright 1945 by Gwendolyn Brooks Blakely; "The Ballad of Rudolph Reed," Copyright © 1960 by Gwendolyn Brooks; and "We Real Cool," Copyright © 1958 by Gwendolyn Brooks, are reprinted from THE WORLD OF GWENDOLYN BROOKS, 1971, by permission of Harper & Row Publishers, Inc. "The Empty Woman" is reprinted from SELECTED POEMS by Gwendolyn Brooks, Copyright © 1963 by Gwendolyn Brooks Blakely, by permission of Harper & Row Publishers, Inc.

LUCILLE CLIFTON. "The 1st" is reprinted from GOOD TIMES by Lucille Clifton. Copyright © 1969 by Lucille Clifton. Reprinted by permission of Random House, Inc.

VICTOR HERNANDEZ CRUZ. "going uptown to visit miriam" is reprinted from SNAPS, by Victor Hernandez Cruz. Copyright © 1968 by Victor Hernandez Cruz. Reprinted by permission of Random House, Inc.

E. E. CUMMINGS. "Buffalo Bill's Defunct" is copyright 1923, 1951 by e. e. cummings. Reprinted from his volume POEMS 1923–1954 by permission of Harcourt Brace Jovanovich, Inc.

EMILY DICKINSON. "Because I Could Not Stop for Death" and "I Heard a Fly Buzz—When I Died," is reprinted by permission of the publisher and the Trustees of Amherst College from Thomas H. Johnson, Editor, THE POEMS OF EMILY DICKINSON, Cambridge, Mass.: The Belknap Press of Harvard University Press, Copyright 1951, 1955 by the President and Fellows of Harvard College.

GERALD DUFF. "The Deep Breather" is reprinted by permission of the author.

RANDY DUNAGAN. "Senior Citizens' City" is reprinted by permission of The World Publishing Company from STUFF edited by Herbert Kohl and Victor Hernandez Cruz. Copyright © 1970 by Herbert Kohl and Victor Hernandez Cruz.

PAUL LAURENCE DUNBAR. "We Wear the Mask" is reprinted by permission of Dodd, Mead & Company, Inc. from THE COMPLETE POEMS OF PAUL LAURENCE DUNBAR.

RAY DUREM. "Award" by Ray Durem is reprinted from NEW NEGRO POETS: USA, edited by Langston Hughes. Copyright © 1964 by Langston Hughes. Reprinted by permission of Indiana University Press.

(continued on page 211)

To Students and Instructors

This book isn't intended to be the last—or the latest—word on poetry. We haven't tried to say things that have never been said before. Instead, we have tried to say some of the first things about poetry, and to encourage the reader to come to his own conclusions. To help make this possible, *Starting with Poetry* includes many poems that have never appeared in a textbook before. We decided to include them because we feel that they represent the living reality of poetry today. New poetry, however, doesn't replace old poetry; it adds to it. For this reason, we have also included older poems. The sections titled "Response" encourage readers to write their own poems, in part to increase their understanding of other poets' techniques, and in part to help them discover their own "poetic vision."

We also hope this book will reveal our own basic assumptions about poetry and will make our values come alive for the reader. The most basic assumption of the book is that poetry is a good thing—that it gives varying degrees of pleasure and by doing so makes its claim as a significant part of human life. Another assumption is that poetry, by focusing and intensifying our insights, is one means by which human beings can become more themselves, more aware of their own minds and places in the world.

Because this book is a beginning, it leaves out more than it includes and thus leaves much for readers to discover on their own. Rather arbitrarily, we have for the most part ruled out the use of translations, since this seemed to raise problems both too large and too specialized for the book as we conceive it. Perhaps the biggest problem about translations is that poems from other cultures may seem more obscure than they really are when presented out of context, and we wanted a selection of poetry that seemed immediate and intelligible in terms of twentieth-century American experience. Readers who are fortunate enough to know a second language—or whose first language is not English—have another poetic world available to them. We have, however, included translations of traditional American Indian poetry because these poems served our purposes very well. Where necessary we have provided some clues to the cultural context in our discussion of the poems.

Music is another large area that can be explored outside the book. Most songs are fatally injured by separating words from music, and thus we have chosen more "literary" than musical ballads and lyrics. This choice is not meant to imply a judgment of quality; the combination of words and music has a vitality that simply cannot be fairly represented through print alone— here the student must turn to the radio, the record player, and the concert.

If our readers take our limitations for their own and stop exploring concepts wherever this book drops them, then we have failed in our primary purpose. The book attempts to stimulate rather than satisfy. It is to be subtracted from, added to, and argued with as its readers' needs and interests require. In the simplest sense, this means that "Responses" can sometimes be skipped, and other poems brought to class. If each student accumulates his "Responses" (and other writing) in a folder or a notebook, he will build up the beginnings of a poetry book of his own. Also, more information about the life and works of particular poets can be pursued separately according to the reader's own interest.

Throughout this book we include photographs we like, as we do poems we like. None of these pictures illustrates a particular poem. They are intended to generate ideas for reader "Responses" and to serve as reminders that there are other mediums for the expression of the reader's own consciousness.

One final point. In almost all writing, pronouns are a problem—who is speaking, and to whom? When we say "we," we refer first of all to ourselves, two particular people, and, beyond ourselves, to a group we try to represent—a variety of average readers who like poetry, are sometimes baffled by it, sometimes believe they see something very clearly, and sometimes know that they need to perceive more clearly still. When we say "you," we are referring to the person using this book. "We" and "you" are not opposites, not enemies.

We would like to thank Jo Anne Moody of Vanderbilt University, John C. Lovas of Foothill College, Ray Liedlich of Portland Community College, Deanne K. Milan of City College, San Francisco, and William Everson for their helpful comments and thoughtful encouragement in our undertaking. We would also like to thank Dianne Kilmer for her valuable advice and suggestions on the picture program.

ANN C. COLLEY and JUDITH K. MOORE

Contents

To Students and Instructors   iii

1 *Poems for a Beginning*   1

ISHMAEL REED   **Beware: Do Not Read This Poem**   1
RESPONSE 1   2
LANGSTON HUGHES   **Ballad of the Landlord**   4
GARY SNYDER   **Hay for the Horses**   5
VACHEL LINDSAY   **The Flower-Fed Buffaloes**   6
RESPONSE 2   6
ROBERT HAYDEN   **The Whipping**   7
RESPONSE 3   10
RESPONSE 4   10
GWENDOLYN BROOKS   **a song in the front yard**   10
LUCILLE CLIFTON   **The 1st**   11
WALT WHITMAN   **from *Song of Myself***   11
TED OLSON   **Mending a Sidewalk . . . Making a Poem**   12

Poems to read and discuss   14

ROBERT VAN DIAS   **Dump Poem**   14
WILLIAM SHAKESPEARE   **Sonnet 55**   14
DENISE LEVERTOV   **The Secret**   15
NANCY WILLARD   **The Graffiti Poet**   16
JOHN KEATS   **A Fragment**   17
LOUIS SIMPSON   **American Poetry**   18
ETHERIDGE KNIGHT   **For Black Poets Who Think of Suicide**   18
FRANCES McCONNEL   **Here I am . . .**   18
NIKKI GIOVANNI   **For Saundra**   20

2 *Sounds*

RICHARD W. THOMAS   **The Worker**   21
RESPONSE 5   21
RESPONSE 6   23
ADELAIDE CRAPSEY   **November Night**   24
BURTON RAFFEL   **On Watching the Construction of a Skyscraper**   24

JAMES TATE **Flight**   25
RESPONSE 7   26
RESPONSE 8   28
ROBERT BLY **Sleet Storm on the Merritt Parkway**   28
ROBERT HAYDEN **Idol**   29
HERMAN MELVILLE **Shiloh**   29
GWENDOLYN BROOKS **We Real Cool**   30
GWENDOLYN BROOKS **The Empty Woman**   31
RESPONSE 9   32
EMILY DICKINSON **Because I Could Not Stop for Death**   33
WALT WHITMAN **When I Heard the Learn'd Astronomer**   35

Poems to read and discuss   36

ROBERT FROST **"Out, Out—"**   36
VERN RUTSALA **Listening**   37
JOHN KNOEPFLE **October scrimmage**   38
EMILY DICKINSON **I Heard a Fly Buzz—When I Died**   38
EDWARD LUCIE-SMITH **Silence**   39
JOHN UPDIKE **Sonic Boom**   39
AL YOUNG **The Curative Powers of Silence**   40
WALT WHITMAN **A Noiseless Patient Spider**   41
AMERICAN INDIAN, NAVAJO, TRADITIONAL **Twelfth Song of the
Thunder**   42
JOHN DRYDEN **Song for Saint Cecilia's Day, 1687**   43
MARGE PIERCY **The Consumer**   44
THOMAS HARDY **During Wind and Rain**   45
WILLIAM BLAKE **London**   46
RAY DUREM **Award**   47
SAMUEL TAYLOR COLERIDGE **Kubla Khan**   47
RAY PATTERSON **You Are the Brave**   49
WILFRED OWEN **Arms and the Boy**   49
THEODORE ROETHKE **My Papa's Waltz**   52
EDMUND SPENSER **Prothalamion**   52

3 *Rhythms*   57

PATRICIA WATSON **Lament for a Brother**   58
RESPONSE 10   59
PATRICIA PARKER **Assassination**   59
JOHN N. MORRIS **The Dream in the City**   60
WILLIAM WORDSWORTH **The World is Too Much with Us**   60
W. H. AUDEN **Who's Who**   61
MERRILL MOORE **How She Resolved to Act**   62
RESPONSE 11   63
A. E. HOUSMAN **To an Athlete Dying Young**   64
RESPONSE 12   65

ROBERT HERRICK **Delight in Disorder**   66
WILLIAM WORDSWORTH **Sonnet Composed upon Westminster
  Bridge**   67
RESPONSE 13   68
ADELAIDE CRAPSEY **Triad**   68

Poems to read and discuss   69

DONNA WHITEWING **August 24, 1963—1:00 A.M.—Omaha**   69
THEODORE ROETHKE **Night Journey**   69
LEROI JONES **Preface to a Twenty Volume Suicide Note**   70
JONATHAN SWIFT **A Satirical Elegy on the Death of a Late
  Famous General**   71
WILLIAM BLAKE **"Nurse's Song," from *Songs of Innocence***   72
              "Nurse's Song," from *Songs of Experience*   72
VICTOR HERNANDEZ CRUZ **going uptown to visit miriam**   73
DON L. LEE **But He Was Cool or: he even stopped for green
  lights**   75
JOHN LACHS **Father**   76
EDWARD S. SPRIGGS **For the TRUTH (because it is necessary)**   76
PHIL GEORGE **Ambition**   77
GERALD DUFF **The Deep Breather**   77
ROBERT HAYDEN **Runagate Runagate**   78

4 *Details: Sights, Smells, Textures*   83

DENISE LEVERTOV **A Day Begins**   83
RESPONSE 14   84
TOM POOLE **I Wonder Why**   84
ROBERT HAYDEN **Market**   85
RANDY DUNAGAN **Senior citizens' city**   87
RESPONSE 15   88
JONATHAN SWIFT **A Description of the Morning**   88
T. S. ELIOT **Morning at the Window**   89
EUGENE McCARTHY **Saturday**   90
RESPONSE 16   90
EUGENE McCARTHY **Bicycle Rider (to Mary)**   91
JOHN LACHS **Houses**   91
RESPONSE 17   92
COLEMAN BARKS **Big Toe**   92
              Cavities   92
              Appendix   92
              Goosepimples   93
              Bruises   93
THEODORE ROETHKE **Dolor**   93
DON L. LEE **Mixed Sketches**   94
RESPONSE 18   96

WILLIAM CARLOS WILLIAMS Young Woman at a Window   96
CAROL FREEMAN Christmas morning i   97
RESPONSE 19   97
VERN RUTSALA Other Lives   97
PATRICIA PARKER Sometimes My Husband   99
JACI EARLEY One Thousand Nine Hundred & Sixty-Eight
Winters   100
RESPONSE 20   100

Poems to read and discuss   101

DONALD HALL The Man in the Dead Machine   101
DAVID HENDERSON Number 5—December   102
MARGE PIERCY The Crippling   102
EDGAR LEE MASTERS Harry Wilmans   103
KATHLEEN FRASER Poem in Which My Legs Are Accepted   104
AMERICAN INDIAN, AZTEC, TRADITIONAL A Woman's Complaint 106
JONATHAN SWIFT A Beautiful Young Nymph Going to Bed   106
CLARENCE MAJOR The Doll Believers   108
MARGARET ATWOOD Game After Supper   108
ALEXANDER POPE Epistle to Miss Blount, on Her Leaving
the Town After the Coronation   109
JAMES TATE Stray Animals   110
MARGE PIERCY morning half-life blues   111
DYLAN THOMAS The Hunchback in the Park   112
WILLIAM J. HARRIS Samantha Is My Negro Cat   114
FRANK LAMONT PHILLIPS When It Was Cold   115
FRANCES McCONNEL Highway 5 Toward Vancouver   116
WILLIAM SHAKESPEARE Sonnet 130   117
WILFRED OWEN Disabled   117
JAMES SEAY Options   119

5 Shapes   121

MARGARET ECKMAN He Returned from the Mine   121
RESPONSE 21   122
JULIUS LESTER Parents   122
The War—II   123
WILLIAM CARLOS WILLIAMS Poem   126
DENISE LEVERTOV Merritt Parkway   126
GEORGE HERBERT Easter Wings   128
JOE GONCALVES Now the Time Is Ripe to Be   129
RESPONSE 22   130
NIKKI GIOVANNI Alabama Poem   130
CHAD WALSH Port Authority Terminal: 9 a.m. Monday   131
THERL RYAN Autumn Woman   133
DON L. LEE Big Momma   134

RESPONSE 23   135
TRADITIONAL BALLAD Bonnie George Campbell   136
LANGSTON HUGHES Could Be   137
RESPONSE 24   138
JOHN KEATS On the Grasshopper and Cricket   139
WILLIAM SHAKESPEARE Sonnet 73   139
EDNA ST. VINCENT MILLAY Sonnet 16   140
MERRILL MOORE Old men and old women going home on the
  street car   141
WILLIAM CARLOS WILLIAMS Smell!   142
T. S. ELIOT Aunt Helen   143
RESPONSE 25   144

Poems to read and discuss   145

DYLAN THOMAS Do Not Go Gentle into That Good Night   145
KENNETH PATCHEN Pleasantly We Shall Remain   146
  I Have a Funny Feeling   146
  The Birds Are Very Careful of This World   147
  He's Either Going Away or Coming Back   147
JOHN UPDIKE The Menagerie at Versailles in 1775   148
D. M. BLACK The Educators   148
NIKKI GIOVANNI Master Charge Blues   150
SAMUEL DANIEL Sonnet 45   150
JUDITH K. MOORE For a High-School Commencement   151
MARGARET ATWOOD Dreams of the Animals   152
LOUIS SIMPSON Carentan O Carentan   153
GWENDOLYN BROOKS The Ballad of Rudolph Reed   155
ROBERT FROST The Fear   157
JOHN MILTON Sonnet 12   160
PAUL LAURENCE DUNBAR We Wear the Mask   161
JAMES SHIRLEY Death the Leveller   161
EDWARD FIELD Unwanted   162
ROY FISHER The Hospital in Winter   163
AL YOUNG Birthday Poem   164
ELIZABETH BISHOP Sestina   165
MICHAEL HARPER We Assume   166
ANONYMOUS Lydia Sherman is Plagued with Rats   167
WILLIAM J. HARRIS My Friend, Wendell Berry   167
W. H. AUDEN Miss Gee   168
E. E. CUMMINGS Buffalo Bill's Defunct   171
EDWARD LEAR The Owl and the Pussy-Cat   173

6 Expectations and Surprises   175
RESPONSE 26   175
ALFRED, LORD TENNYSON The Sleeping Beauty   176

DAVID LAWSON No Great Matter   177
AMERICAN INDIAN, TRADITIONAL The Whole World Is Coming   179
OLIVER GOLDSMITH Song   179
RESPONSE 27   181
WALTER SAVAGE LANDOR On His Seventy-fifth Birthday   181
WILLIAM WORDSWORTH My Heart Leaps Up   181
PERCY BYSSHE SHELLEY The Indian Serenade   182
LEROI JONES For Hettie   183
WILLIAM COLLINS Ode Written in the Beginning of the Year
1746   184
WILFRED OWEN Anthem for Doomed Youth   184
ROBERT HAYDEN Snow   185
RESPONSE 28   185

Poems to read and discuss   187

JOHN DRYDEN "Song," from *Marriage a la Mode*   187
AL YOUNG A Dance for Militant Dilettantes   188
AUDRE LORDE Naturally   189
THEODORE ROETHKE Vernal Sentiment   189
ETHERIDGE KNIGHT Crazy Pigeon   190
WILLIAM J. HARRIS A Winter Song   190
JAMES WELCH The Man from Washington   191
          Christmas Comes to Moccasin Flat   192
JOHN UPDIKE How to Be Uncle Sam   192
EVE MERRIAM Ding, Dong, Bell   194
          Fee, Fi, Fo, Fum   194
          Wino Will   194
ELIZABETH BISHOP Manners   195
DICK LOURIE Wash. Rinse. Dry.   196
HYACINTHE HILL Rebels from Fairy Tales   198
RICHARD EBERHART For a Lamb   198
WILLIAM BUTLER YEATS Politics   199
THOMAS GRAY On the Death of a Favourite Cat   199

7 *What Finally Matters*   201
DEREK MAHON My Wicked Uncle   202
AL YOUNG Lonesome in the Country   204
ROBERT HERSHON Spitting on Ira Rosenblatt   204

APPENDIX
HOW TO WRITE ABOUT POETRY   206

INDEX   209

1

Poems
for a Beginning

BEWARE: DO NOT READ THIS POEM

tonite, thriller was
abt an ol woman, so vain she
surrounded herself w/
   many mirrors

it got so bad that finally she
locked herself indoors & her
whole life became the
   mirrors

one day the villagers broke
into her house, but she was too   10
swift for them. she disappeared
   into a mirror
each tenant who bought the house
after that, lost a loved one to
   the ol woman in the mirror:
   first a little girl
   then a young woman
   then the young woman/s husband

the hunger of this poem is legendary
it has taken in many victims   20
back off from this poem
it has drawn in yr feet
back off from this poem
it has drawn in yr legs

back off from this poem
it is a greedy mirror
you are into this poem from
        the waist down
nobody can hear you can they?
this poem has had you up to here   30
        belch
this poem aint got no manners
you cant call out frm this poem
relax now & go w/ this poem
move & roll on to this poem
do not resist this poem
this poem has yr eyes
this poem has his head
this poem has his arms
this poem has his fingers   40
this poem has his fingertips

this poem is the reader & the
reader this poem.

statistic: the us bureau of missing persons reports
            that in 1968 over 100,000 people disappeared
            leaving no solid clues
                        nor trace   only
        a space   in the lives of their friends

                                        ISHMAEL REED

Response 1

Starting with the title, what do you feel when you are told to beware
of reading Ishmael Reed's poem? Quickly, without worrying about it,
write down some of your reactions to the poem.

   What you have written probably tells more about your personal
involvement with this particular poem than about an abstraction called

"poetry." Use what you have written to begin a notebook or folder in which you collect your personal responses to the poems you read in this book. Sometimes we will ask you for specific responses, but there is no limit to what you can include. Your notebook can become a sort of diary of your unique relationship—sometimes good, sometimes bad —with poetry.

Ishmael Reed doesn't give his readers a definition of poetry. Instead, he involves the reader in a specific poem so that the powers of poetry can be sensed by each individual. One of the best ways for a reader to express his experience of what a poem does is to compare the poem to a prose statement. This way, a reader can begin to recognize for himself those characteristic qualities that make a piece of writing poetry.

BALLAD OF THE LANDLORD

Landlord, landlord,
My roof has sprung a leak.
Don't you 'member I told you about it
Way last week?

Landlord, landlord,
These steps is broken down.
When you come up yourself
It's a wonder you don't fall down.

Ten Bucks you say I owe you?
Ten Bucks you say is due?   10
Well, that's Ten Bucks more'n I'll pay you
Till you fix this house up new.

What? You gonna get eviction orders?
You gonna cut off my heat?
You gonna take my furniture and
Throw it in the street?

Um-huh! You talking high and mighty.
Talk on—till you get through.
You ain't gonna be able to say a word
If I land my fist on you.   20

Police! Police!
Come and get this man!
He's trying to ruin the government
And overturn the land!

Copper's whistle!
Patrol bell!
Arrest.

Precinct Station.
Iron cell.
Headlines in press: 30

MAN THREATENS LANDLORD

                              •

                        •   •

TENANT HELD NO BAIL

                        •

                  •   •

JUDGE GIVES NEGRO 90 DAYS IN COUNTY JAIL
                              LANGSTON HUGHES

HAY FOR THE HORSES

He had driven half the night
From far down San Joaquin
Through Mariposa, up the
Dangerous mountain roads,
And pulled in at eight a.m.
With his big truckload of hay
            behind the barn.
With winch and ropes and hooks
We stacked the bales up clean
To splintery redwood rafters   10
High in the dark, flecks of alfalfa
Whirling through shingle-cracks of light,

Itch of haydust in the
            sweaty shirt and shoes.
At lunchtime under Black oak
Out in the hot corral,
—The old mare nosing lunchpails,
Grasshoppers crackling in the weeds—
"I'm sixty-eight" he said,
"I first bucked hay when I was seventeen   20
I thought, that day I started,
I sure would hate to do this all my life
And dammit, that's just what
I've gone and done."

                                    GARY SNYDER

THE FLOWER-FED BUFFALOES

The flower-fed buffaloes of the spring
In the days of long ago,
Ranged where the locomotives sing
And the prairie flowers lie low:—
The tossing, blooming, perfumed grass
Is swept away by the wheat,
Wheels and wheels and wheels spin by
In the spring that still is sweet.
But the flower-fed buffaloes of the spring
Left us, long ago.   10
They gore no more, they bellow no more,
They trundle around the hills no more:—
With the Blackfeet, lying low.
With the Pawnees, lying low,
Lying low.

                        VACHEL LINDSAY

Response 2

Without reading any further, choose one of the three poems printed
above that you like best. Translate it into a prose version—a few
sentences or a short paragraph.

Compare your prose version with the original. What has happened to the physical shape of the poem on the page? In what way do the two versions affect you differently? What, in the poem, helps to create its effect and convey its meaning? In your mind, what distinguishes the poem from the prose?

Compare your results with those of other students. You might like to discuss your reactions in small groups, if that is possible.

THE WHIPPING

The old woman across the way
    is whipping the boy again
and shouting to the neighborhood
    her goodness and his wrongs.

Wildly he crashes through elephant ears,
    pleads in dusty zinnias,
while she in spite of crippling fat
    pursues and corners him.

She strikes and strikes the shrilly circling
    boy till the stick breaks   10
in her hand. His tears are rainy weather
    to woundlike memories:

My head gripped in bony vise
    of knees, the writhing struggle
to wrench free, the blows, the fear
    worse than blows that hateful

Words could bring, the face that I
    no longer knew or loved . . .
Well, it is over now, it is over,
    and the boy sobs in his room,   20

And the woman leans muttering against
    a tree, exhausted, purged—
avenged in part for lifelong hidings
    she has had to bear.

        ROBERT HAYDEN

POEMS FOR A BEGINNING

A prose version of "The Whipping" will probably go something like this:

> The old woman across the street is whipping her boy again, shouting as she does so. He cries and attempts to escape, but she captures him, beating him so severely that the stick breaks. His misery reminds me of similar events in my own childhood. When the whipping is over, the boy cries in his room and the woman, worn out but satisfied, leans resting against a tree.

Even a detailed prose paraphrase will probably seem shorter than the poem. It sits on the page like a brick, the lines ending where the right-hand margin, rather than the author, dictates. The poem's lines, on the other hand, form a pattern created by the poet through the placement of his words, the lines ending where he wants them to. The pattern of words and lines can influence a reader's response in many ways. One instance of this in "The Whipping" occurs in the third stanza:

> She strikes and strikes the shrilly circling
>   boy till the stick breaks
> in her hand.

The line breaks as the stick does, because the poet has shaped his poem to reinforce his meaning.

While the prose version conveys essentially the same facts, the poem appeals more directly to the emotions, even calling for a response from the reader's body. "His misery reminds me of similar events in my own childhood" is clear but very general. The poem tells more than the facts—it tells how the facts felt and moves the reader to feel them too. The poetic way of stating these facts, "My head gripped in bony vise / of knees, the writhing struggle / to wrench free," tightens the reader's muscles with sympathy.

The poem's sound patterns, or rhythms, help to involve the reader in its action also. When we read aloud, "She strikes and strikes," we find ourselves emphasizing "strikes," suggesting the repeated blows of the stick itself and the determined energy of the woman. The phrase describing the boy's "writhing struggle / to wrench free" helps to convey the tension and breathless anxiety that the boy feels in his terrified attempt to escape the beating. It does this partly through the brief pause between the two lines and the essential pause between "wrench" and "free" as the reader's mouth moves from the shape of one sound to that of another.

Response 3

These few examples of how "The Whipping" works suggest many more. In your notebook, jot down some of the questions and ideas that reading the poem has brought up for you.

Here are some of the questions that have occurred to us. What sort of setting is created by the phrases "elephant ears" and "dusty zinnias"? Why does the poet introduce the word "My" at the beginning of the fourth stanza, and what does that tell about his involvement in what he is describing? What is suggested—not stated—by the lines "His tears are rainy weather / to woundlike memories," and how does it differ from our paraphrase?

Questions like these, once we learn to ask them, can be endless; learning to raise them is as important as discovering answers to them. Ask yourself, for instance, about the repetition of the initial *w* sound throughout "The Whipping." What meanings does it have for you? Some readers will see many, while others may see only a few.

Response 4

Once again try to paraphrase in prose one of the following three poems, using our version of "The Whipping" as a model.

A SONG IN THE FRONT YARD

I've stayed in the front yard all my life.
I want a peek at the back
Where it's rough and untended and hungry weed grows.
A girl gets sick of a rose.

I want to go in the back yard now
And maybe down the alley,
To where the charity children play.
I want a good time today.

They do some wonderful things.
They have some wonderful fun.   10
My mother sneers, but I say it's fine
How they don't have to go in at quarter to nine.

My mother, she tells me that Johnnie Mae
Will grow up to be a bad woman.
That George'll be taken to Jail soon or late
(On account of last winter he sold our back gate).

But I say it's fine. Honest, I do.
And I'd like to be a bad woman, too,
And wear the brave stockings of night-black lace
And strut down the streets with paint on my face.   20

GWENDOLYN BROOKS

THE 1st

What I remember about that day
is boxes stacked across the walk
and couch springs curling through the air
and drawers and tables balanced on the curb
and us, hollering,
leaping up and around
happy to have a playground;

nothing about the emptied rooms
nothing about the emptied family

LUCILLE CLIFTON

from SONG OF MYSELF

I think I could turn and live with animals, they're so placid and
    self-contain'd,
I stand and look at them long and long.
They do not sweat and whine about their condition,
They do not lie awake in the dark and weep for their sins,
They do not make me sick discussing their duty to God,
Not one is dissatisfied, not one is demented with the mania of
    owning things,
Not one kneels to another, nor to his kind that lived thousands
    of years ago,
Not one is respectable or unhappy over the whole earth.

WALT WHITMAN

As our discussion of Robert Hayden's "The Whipping" and your experiences with Response 4 show, readers can isolate certain elements that are important in poetry: sounds, rhythmic patterns, vividly observed and presented details. And readers can also see some of the ways these elements work—in particular the patterning of lines and the playing with the reader's expectations. Studying these elements separately, however, is only a beginning. What finally matters is to pull the separate parts together into one coherent experience. When the reader does this, he parallels what the poet himself has done. Ted Olson uses a description of mending a sidewalk to explain how he goes about writing a poem. While the basic ingredients are essential, and there are even certain formulas for combining them, neither ingredients nor formulas can automatically make a poem.

MENDING A SIDEWALK . . . MAKING A POEM

It's simple in theory. Just three ingredients:
something solid, something fluid, some sort of binder.
The mix, though, must be right. The formulas
never quite fit. You keep experimenting:
a cupful, a fistful, a sprinkle. But look out:
a slosh too much and it's ruined.
                  Now to work.
They're refractory. They sulk. They don't want to marry.
You thwack, pummel, flail, churn, larrup,
and cuss. You're tempted to say the hell with it.   10
But somehow finally they cohere, into an ugly
coarse gray sludge.
              And that's just the beginning.
The stuff doesn't like being caged. It clots, clogs,
spills over, goes wherever it isn't supposed to.
Matter's contrary. You've got to show it you're boss.
And slowly, ever so slowly, it dociles. You think
By golly, I've got it! But you haven't. Not yet.
It has to jell. Don't try to hurry it. But don't
wait too long. Catch it while it's malleable.   20

Now to groom and polish. Carefully . . . carefully . . .
until at last the coarse gray-burlap surface
takes on grain and lustre.
              Stop, now, quick!
Don't let it get too slick.

                      TED OLSON

So far, we have stressed the techniques the poet uses to communicate an experience or an idea to his readers. To most of us, however, it is the subject matter of the poem—the experience or idea—which makes the most immediate appeal. A late movie on television, a fight with the landlord, memories of childhood, buffaloes ranging on the prairie are all possible subjects for poetry, and they appeal differently to different readers. Unfortunately, many people think that the topics "suitable" for poetry are limited to a few, mainly love, nature, and death. Not only is this notion false, as a look at just the poems included in this chapter will show, but it misrepresents poetry so greatly that many readers narrow their expectations and therefore get much less pleasure than they might.

If the subject of a poem has personal meaning for you, this makes the poem naturally appealing, but it may ultimately disappoint you if the poem fails to do justice to its subject. How the poet presents and arranges what he has to say finally influences your reaction to his poem.

This chapter ends with nine very different poems on the subject of poetry. When you read them, try to decide which ones you like the most. Then try to explain why. Take into account both what the poets say and how they say it.

Poems
to read and discuss

DUMP POEM

This is a genuine used poem
last-year's model poem
shirt off someone's back poem
chair minus a leg poem
scrap husk and rind poem
steakbone poem.
You can smell this poem when the wind is right
for miles, around it swoop
herring gulls and great-black-backed gulls,
leaves of a rainsoaked paperback now dry   10
flutter around it, and graffiti of stripped wallpaper.
This poem is to be thrown out
sprinkled with kerosene
set afire so you can hear its juices
sizzling and its light bulbs popping:
bulldozed, buried, used for fill.

ROBERT VAN DIAS

SONNET 55

Not marble, nor the gilded monuments
Of princes, shall outlive this pow'rful rhyme,
But you shall shine more bright in these contents
Than unswept stone, besmeared with sluttish time.
When wasteful war shall statues overturn,
And broils root out the work of masonry,

Nor Mars his sword nor war's quick fire shall burn
The living record of your memory.
'Gainst death and all oblivious enmity
Shall you pace forth; your praise shall still find room   10
Even in the eyes of all posterity
That wear this world out to the ending doom.
  So, till the judgment that yourself arise,
  You live in this, and dwell in lovers' eyes.

WILLIAM SHAKESPEARE

THE SECRET

Two girls discover
the secret of life
in a sudden line of
poetry.

I who don't know the
secret wrote
the line. They
told me

(through a third person)
they had found it   10
but not what it was
not even

what line it was. No doubt
by now, more than a week
later, they have forgotten
the secret,

the line, the name of
the poem. I love them
for finding what
I can't find,   20

and for loving me
for the line I wrote,
and for forgetting it
so that

a thousand times, till death
finds them, they may
discover it again, in other
lines

in other
happenings. And for   30
wanting to know it,
for

assuming there is
such a secret, yes,
for that
most of all.

> DENISE LEVERTOV

THE GRAFFITI POET

I grew up in the schoolrooms of the Dakotas,
I sat by the wood stove and longed for spring.
My desk leaned like a clavichord, stripped of its hammers,
and on it I carved my name, forever and ever,
so the seed of that place should never forget me.
Outside, in their beehive tombs, I could hear
the dead spinning extravagant honey.
I remembered their names and wanted only
that the living remember mine.

I am the invisible student, dead end   10
of a crowded class. I write and nobody answers.
On the Brooklyn Bridge, I wrote a poem:
the rain washed it away.
On the walls of the Pentagon, I made
My sign; a workman blasted me off like dung.
From the halls of Newark to the shores
of Detroit, I engrave my presence with fire
so the lords of those places may never forget me.

Save me. I can hardly speak. So we pass,
not speaking. In bars where your dreams drink,   20
I scrawl your name, my name, in a heart
that the morning daily erases.
At Dachau, at Belsen I blazoned my cell
with voices and saw my poem sucked
into a single cry:
throw me a fistful of stars.
I died writing, as the walls fell.

I am lonely. More than any monument,
I want you to see me writing: *I love
you* (or someone), *I live* (or you live).   30
Canny with rancour, with love, I teach you
to spell, to remember your name
and your epitaphs which are always changing.
Listen to me, stranger, keep me alive.
                    I am you.
                    NANCY WILLARD

A FRAGMENT

Where's the Poet? show him! show him,
Muses nine! that I may know him!
'Tis the man who with a man
    Is an equal, be he King,
Or poorest of the beggar-clan,
    Or any other wondrous thing
A man may be 'twixt ape and Plato;
    'Tis the man who with a bird,
Wren or Eagle, finds his way to
    All its instincts; he hath heard   10
The Lion's roaring, and can tell
    What his horny throat expresseth,
And to him the Tiger's yell
    Comes articulate and presseth
On his ear like mother-tongue.
                    JOHN KEATS

AMERICAN POETRY

Whatever it is, it must have
A stomach that can digest
Rubber, coal, uranium, moons, poems.

Like the shark, it contains a shoe.
It must swim for miles through the desert
Uttering cries that are almost human.

                                        LOUIS SIMPSON

FOR BLACK POETS
WHO THINK OF SUICIDE

Black Poets should live—not leap
From steel bridges (like the white boys do.
Black Poets should *live*—not lay
Their necks on railroad tracks (like the white boys do.
Black Poets should seek—but not search too much
In sweet dark caves, nor hunt for snipes
Down psychic trails (like the white boys do.

For Black Poets belong to Black People. Are
The Flutes of Black Lovers. Are
The Organs of Black Sorrows. Are   10
The Trumpets of Black Warriors.
Let all Black Poets die as trumpets,
And be buried in the dust of marching feet.

                                        ETHERIDGE KNIGHT

HERE I AM . . .

Here I am in a new poem.
Does it become
me? Pull down your skirt,
says a critic.
I like you better
in bluegreen and songbirds.
Talk goes around that she's dressed
in no bra at all.

I protest,
it's a grownup poem. I'll   10
reveal what I want to.
But embarrassed
I straighten the seams
though the lines
are alive in a kind of disorder
I despair of revising.
I despair of the cloth,
threadbare and binding,
and ask myself: why
do you wear on your heart
this thin sleeve of a poem   20
as if nobody could love you
for yourself without rhyme,
yourself only?

      FRANCES McCONNEL

FOR SAUNDRA

i wanted to write
a poem
that rhymes
but revolution doesn't lend
itself to be-bopping

then my neighbor
who thinks i hate
asked—do you ever write
tree poems—i like trees
so i thought   10
i'll write a beautiful green tree poem
peeked from my window
to check the image
noticed the school yard was covered
with asphalt
no green—no trees grow
in manhattan

then, well, i thought the sky
i'll do a big blue sky poem
but all the clouds have winged   20
low since no-Dick was elected

so i thought again
and it occurred to me
maybe i shouldn't write
at all
but clean my gun
and check my kerosene supply

perhaps these are not poetic
times
at all   30

                    NIKKI GIOVANNI

2
Sounds

Diddle diddle dumpling, my son John,
Went to bed with his stockings on
One shoe off and one shoe on;
Diddle diddle dumpling, my son John.

A child hears a nursery rhyme and responds to its sound and rhythms
long before he learns to read it silently or to comprehend the meanings
of the words. His pleasure in the nursery rhyme he doesn't "under-
stand" hints that perhaps some of the meaning that adults think they
find only in the words may come from the sounds of the poem as well.

In Richard W. Thomas' poem "The Worker," the sounds of the
words reinforce the contrast between the worker's collapse and the
way the factory continues to function regardless of his suffering. This
contrast is expressed by the opposition of the -ing words (which all
describe activity continu*ing*) and the abruptness of the repeated half-
line, "they couldn't stop." The rather quiet sounds of the words de-
scribing the father "hushed" under "hospital sheets" contrast with the
irritating mechanical noises.

THE WORKER

My father lies black and hushed
Beneath white hospital sheets
He collapsed at work

His iron left him
Slow and quiet he sank
Meeting the wet concrete floor on his way
The wheels were still turning—they couldn't stop
Red and yellow lights flashing
Gloved hands twisting knobs—they couldn't stop
And as they carried him out   10
The whirling and buzzing and humming machines
Applauded him
Lapping up his dripping iron
              They couldn't stop

RICHARD W. THOMAS

The grating mechanical noises in "The Worker" also can be heard in the first line of Robert Frost's poem "Out, Out—" (see page 36): "The buzz saw snarled and rattled in the yard." Here the sounds create a sense of danger and anxiety that prepares the reader for the horrible event that is about to happen, an accident in which a young boy's hand is cut off. "Snarled" goes even further, since animals, and even people, may snarl; the event seems to be not merely an accident but a deliberate act of cruelty.

When we look at the varied kinds of work "snarl" does, we begin to see an advantage that adults have over the two-year-old with his nursery rhymes—for us, the meanings and the sounds of words tend to be fused together and to reinforce each other. Richard W. Thomas' "stop" not only ends lines with the abrupt *p* sound but *means* stop as well. "Twisting" and "whirling" not only signal continuous activity through their -ing endings but also indicate specific kinds of repetitive motion.

Sometimes people protest against the subjectivity of our responses to sound. After all how can we prove that a word like "buzzing" carries all the implications we say it does? We can't, of course, but fortunately we don't have to. We are talking about a reservoir of feelings and implications that the words of our native language have for us because they are our words, words we use every day in an extraordinary variety of ways. An implication may be active in one use and absent in another; crucially important in one, present but unimportant in another.

ℛesponse 5

In order to write "The Worker," Richard W. Thomas first had to be aware of the sounds of the factory and the hospital. Listen to the sounds connected with some of the following things (or reconstruct them in your memory), and write down some of the words that describe, suggest, or even imitate those sounds. If something on the list leaves you cold, omit it and use something else with more interest for you instead.

The room you are in.
One of your relatives.
A car accident.
A laundromat.
A lunch counter.

When you read your results aloud, can others identify what you are describing? What makes your choices work?

Response 6

Choose the group of words from Response 5 that you think best suggests the person, object, or event you have listened to, and try arranging the items in it as a short poem. You can use "November Night" and "On Watching the Construction of a Skyscraper" as models.

NOVEMBER NIGHT

Listen . . .
With faint dry sound,
Like steps of passing ghosts,
The leaves, frost-crisp'd, break from the trees
And fall.

ADELAIDE CRAPSEY

ON WATCHING THE CONSTRUCTION OF A SKYSCRAPER

Nothing sings from these orange trees,
Rindless steel as smooth as sapling skin,
Except a crane's brief wheeze
And all the muffled, clanking din
Of rivets nosing in like bees.

BURTON RAFFEL

While we may isolate one word—like "buzzing" or "whirling"—in order to talk about it, the word in any actual poem, of course, stands in relation to other words. For example, James Tate's poem "Flight, for K." strengthens and qualifies the feelings we get from separate words by the way they relate to each other.

FLIGHT

for K.

Like a glum cricket
the refrigerator is singing
and just as I am convinced

that it is the only noise
in the building, a pot falls
in 2B. The neighbors on

both sides of me suddenly
realize that they have not
made love to their wives

since 1947. The racket   10
multiplies. The man down hall
is teaching his dog to fly.

The fish are disgusted
and beat their heads blue
against a cold aquarium. I too

lose control and consider
the dust huddled in the corner
a threat to my endurance.

Were you here, we would not
tolerate mongrels in the air,   20
nor the conspiracies of dust.

We would drive all night,
your head tilted on my shoulder.
At dawn, I would nudge you

with my anxious fingers and say,
Already we are in Idaho.

JAMES TATE

Because the reader comes upon the refrigerator's "singing" only after the comparison to a "glum cricket" has been made, he knows at once what sort of singing is meant. The soft, quiet *s* sounds in "singing," "just," "convinced," are unexpectedly interrupted by the abrupt "pot" that drops in the middle of the fifth line. The singing of the refrigerator, a sound we only notice in silence, like that of the remembered cricket, evokes a mood of quiet loneliness. But both the sound and the mood are broken by the increasingly preposterous sequence of noises that begins bumpily with:

> a pot falls
> in 2B. The neighbors on
>
> both sides of me suddenly
> realize that they have not
> made love to their wives

"Pot" rhymes unexpectedly with "not," "2B" rhymes with "me" and "suddenly," thus ending the lonely stillness. Indeed, as Tate says, "The racket / multiplies." We can almost hear a senseless thudding as the fish "*b*eat their heads *b*lue / against a *c*old a*q*uarium." "*D*ust" and "hud-*d*led" may well seem threatening and conspiratorial when their sounds build on one another in rapid sequence. Toward the end of the poem there is a return to the *s* sounds, which echoes the opening lines and creates a new quiet: "conspiracies," "dust," "shoulder," "anxious," "fingers," "say."

Response 7

Write a poem whose mood and scene contrast with those of the one you wrote for Response 6. When you read your two poems aloud, do you find that the sounds help to set the tone you wanted? If not, change some of the words to others of similar meaning but more appropriate sound.

If you have trouble writing a poem, write a few lines of prose using the sounds you want your readers to hear.

Sometimes repeated sounds very strongly influence meaning, as for instance in the first two stanzas of Thomas Gray's "Elegy in a Country Churchyard":

> The curfew tolls the knell of parting day,
>   The lowing herd winds slowly o'er the lea,
> The ploughman homeward plods his weary way,
>   And leaves the world to darkness and to me.
>
> Now fades the glimmering landscape on the sight,
>   And all the air a solemn stillness holds,
> Save where the beetle wheels his droning flight,
>   And drowsy tinklings lull the distant folds.

Gray repeats and varies patterns of sound from line to line: "The *pl*oughman homeward *pl*ods"; "The *low*ing herd *w*inds s*low*ly o'er the *l*ea"; "The ploughman home*w*ard plods his *w*eary *w*ay, / And leaves the *w*orld. . . ." Again, "the b*ee*tle wh*ee*ls his *dro*ning flight, / And *dro*wsy tinklings lull"; "a *s*olemn *s*tillnes*s* hold*s*." The *l* sound is repeated twenty-three times in these eight lines. Throughout the two stanzas the *o* sound that is first heard in "tolls" is repeated again and again and modulated many times—"lowing," "slowly," "world," "holds," "droning," "drowsy," "folds."

This sort of word-listing has often discouraged students because it seemed to have no purpose. We always need to ask, What's the point of it all? Look again at those first two stanzas of Gray's "Elegy," in which the end of the day is signalled by the tolling bell. The sounds amplify the poet's chosen visual details; the ploughman "plods," a word that refers to heavy, lagging movement and also echoes in reverse the combination of *o* and *l* sounds in the key word "tolls." Suppose the line read, "The ploughman homeward strolls. . . ." The different meaning of "stroll"—a casual, enjoyable kind of walk—would work against the sound effect of the *o-l* grouping. Sound and meaning work together. The echoes of the tolling bell tend to occur in words whose connotations fit the overall mood of weariness and sadness—"slowly," "droning," "plods"—and the quietness of the end of day is conveyed by the muted sounds of "lowing," "drowsy." We can almost hear the whispery sounds that fill the "solemn stillness."

Response 8

You have probably been reading the poems in this book silently. Even from such reading you can understand some of the effects of sound. To experience them more fully, however, you should read the poems aloud or listen to them being read. Here are three poems full of sounds that intensify meanings. You will probably find you need to practice in order to get them right. If you are not sure how to go about reading a poem aloud, you might listen to one or two of the many records of poetry readings. Listen only, however, to get ideas, not to imitate.

SLEET STORM ON THE MERRITT PARKWAY

I look out at the white sleet covering the still streets
As we drive through Scarsdale—
The sleet began falling as we left Connecticut,
And the winter leaves swirled in the wet air after cars
Like hands suddenly turned over in a conversation.
Now the frost has nearly buried the short grass of March.
Seeing the sheets of sleet untouched on the wide streets,
I think of the many comfortable homes stretching for miles,
Two and three stories, solid, with polished floors,
With white curtains in the upstairs bedrooms,   10

And small perfume flagons of black glass on the window sills,
And warm bathrooms with guest towels, and electric lights—
What a magnificent place for a child to grow up!
And yet the children end in the river of price-fixing,
Or in the snowy field of the insane asylum.
The sleet falls—so many cars moving toward New York—
Last night we argued about the Marines invading Guatemala in
    1947,
The United Fruit Company had one water spigot for 200 fami-
    lies,
And the ideals of America, our freedom to criticize,
The slave systems of Rome and Greece, and no one agreed.   20

ROBERT BLY

IDOL

(Coatlicue, Aztec Goddess)

Wail of the newborn, cry of the dying,
sirenscream of agonies;
    taloned shriek, gong and cymbal of wreckage,
drumbeat of bloodblackened praise;
    soundless drumthrob of the heart wrenched
from the living breast,
    of the raw meaty heart quivering in copal
smoke its praise.

ROBERT HAYDEN

SHILOH.

A Requiem.

(April, 1862.)

Skimming lightly, wheeling still,
    The swallows fly low
Over the field in clouded days,
    The forest-field of Shiloh—
Over the field where April rain
Solaced the parched ones stretched in pain

Through the pause of night
That followed the Sunday fight
  Around the church of Shiloh—
The church so lone, the log-built one, 10
That echoed to many a parting groan
    And natural prayer
    Of dying foemen mingled there—
Foemen at morn, but friends at eve—
    Fame or country least their care:
(What like a bullet can undeceive!)
    But now they lie low,
    While over them the swallows skim.
    And all is hushed at Shiloh.

HERMAN MELVILLE

Continue reading poems aloud as you go through the book, and also try reading your own favorite poems aloud. Some poems are more rewarding than others when approached in this way, but often such reading will increase your understanding as well as your enjoyment.

One sound effect that almost everyone especially connects with poetry is rhyme—although many poems in fact don't rhyme and many poets never write rhyming poems at all. For those who do, there may be many different reasons. Some traditional kinds of poetry require a particular arrangement of rhymes, so if a poet chooses to use one of these kinds, rhyme is a part of his choice. Also, rhyme may be used as other sounds are—to create specific effects. How do the rhymes in the following poem influence your understanding of it?

WE REAL COOL

The Pool Players.
Seven at the Golden Shovel.

We real cool. We
Left school. We

Lurk late. We
Strike straight. We

Sing sin. We
Thin gin. We

Jazz June. We
Die soon.

GWENDOLYN BROOKS

Each line but the last ends with "We," and in addition to this each two-line stanza contains a perfect rhyme: "cool / school," "late / straight," "sin / gin," and "June / soon." It seems to us that the effect of all this rhyming is to make us feel almost as trapped as the pool players at the Golden Shovel. These tight, frequent rhymes help to box the reader into the pool players' situation and also to emphasize their slickness. The absence of "We," the rhyming word we expect to find in the last line, abruptly indicates their early deaths.

Gwendolyn Brooks also uses rhyme powerfully in another poem.

THE EMPTY WOMAN

The empty woman took toys!
   In her sisters' homes
Were little girls and boys.

The empty woman had hats
To show. With feathers. Wore combs
In polished waves. Wooed cats

And pigeons. Shopped.
Shopped hard for nephew-toys,
Niece-toys. Made taffy. Popped

Popcorn and hated her sisters,   10
Featherless and waveless but able to
Mend measles, nag noses, blast blisters

And all day waste wordful girls
And war-boys, and all day
Say "Oh God!"—and tire among curls

And plump legs and proud muscle
And blackened school-bags, babushkas, torn socks,
And bouffants that bustle, and rustle.

GWENDOLYN BROOKS

The brisk rhymes of "toys" and "boys," "hats" and "cats," "shopped"
and "popped" rush the reader through the first three stanzas of the
poem. They are short, crisp words that reflect the tidiness—and ulti-
mately the hollowness—of the childless woman's relationship to her
"featherless and waveless" sisters. The harsh rhymes of the first three
stanzas contrast with the softer, more flowing sounds of the last three,
just as the empty woman's life contrasts with the full ones led by her
sisters. "Sisters" is rhymed with "blisters." Both words, unlike "hats"
and "cats," are two syllables long and have to be pronounced more
slowly. The sounds of "girls" and "curls" can also be prolonged, and
the crowding rhymes of the final stanza, "muscle," "bustle," and
"rustle," also reflect the disorderly, but apparently full, exciting, and
therefore enviable, life of the sisters.

Response 9

Experiment with the possibilities of rhyme by writing new second
lines to some two-line poems. To a great degree you can control
the emotional effect of your two-line poem by your choice of the
rhyming word. For example, suppose you had been given the first
line, "The winter now begins to frown"; you might have written a
second line, "The snow is softly falling down." The first line is by
Jonathan Swift, who set a very different mood by writing as his second
line, "Poor Stella must pack off to town." The frowning winter leads
the reader to expect a nature poem, so the effect of the rhyme-word
"town," being unexpected, is comic. For each of the following lines by
William Blake, compose two or more rhyming second lines in which the
rhyme-word capsulizes the poem's emotional effect. Try to vary your
results as much as possible.

"What is it men in women do require?"
"I dreamt a dream! What can it mean?"

Rhymes, as we have shown, can shape the mood of the poem. They can also imply a certain order, as in the following poem.

BECAUSE I COULD NOT STOP FOR DEATH

Because I could not stop for Death—
He kindly stopped for me—
The Carriage held but just Ourselves—
And Immortality.

We slowly drove—He knew no haste
And I had put away
My labor and my leisure too,
For His Civility—

We passed the School, where Children strove
At Recess—in the Ring—   10
We passed the Fields of Gazing Grain—
We passed the Setting Sun—

Or rather—He passed Us—
The Dews drew quivering and chill—
For only Gossamer, my Gown—
My Tippet—only Tulle—

We paused before a House that seemed
A Swelling of the Ground—
The Roof was scarcely visible—
The Cornice—in the Ground—   20

Since then—'tis Centuries—and yet
Feels shorter than the Day
I first surmised the Horses' Heads
Were toward Eternity—

                    EMILY DICKINSON

Emily Dickinson uses a very conventional rhyme, "me/-ity," a standby of rhyming poets for centuries, in her first stanza in order to create a familiar frame to hold a bizarre statement. The rhyme also orders the poem by linking the poet's self, "me," to the huge abstractions "Immortality," "Civility," and "Eternity." She uses approximate rhymes—a repeated vowel plus "n" in "ring/Grain/Sun"—to parallel the rapidly passing scene outside the carriage window, while the thump of "Ground/Ground" in the fifth stanza suggests the finality of the grave. The placing of "than the Day" and "Eternity" at the ends of the second and fourth lines in the final stanza—where we expect to find rhyming words—is both close to rhyme in sound and different enough to suggest the disparity between the short time span and the endless one and the idea that the endlessness of eternity can still be thought of as one infinitely expanding day.

Even though Gwendolyn Brooks' and Emily Dickinson's rhymes do different things, they both make the poem concise and build a set of limits to enclose the reader. When Walt Whitman decided to write about a subject related to Emily Dickinson's, he wanted to give his poem a feeling of openness and expansion, so he rejected rhyme and instead used lines—often long ones—of roughly parallel form. The poem has no rhymes and consequently seems more open and expansive than the rhymed poems you have just read.

WHEN I HEARD THE LEARN'D ASTRONOMER

When I heard the learn'd astronomer,
When the proofs, the figures, were ranged in columns before
   me,
When I was shown the charts and diagrams, to add, divide,
   and measure them,
When I sitting heard the astronomer where he lectured with
   much applause in the lecture-room,
How soon unaccountable I became tired and sick,
Till rising and gliding out I wander'd off by myself,
In the mystical moist night-air, and from time to time,
Look'd up in perfect silence at the stars.

WALT WHITMAN

When you read the following poems, first isolate the different sounds and then explain how the poet uses them to support the meaning or mood of his poem. There is usually more than one value to a sound in a poem, but never forget that many sounds are present mainly because the writer found them pleasing to his own ear. It isn't necessary to invent an explanation for everything.

Also, just because these poems all have interesting uses of sound doesn't mean that they have no other value, or that other poems in later chapters aren't worth considering for their use of sound. We single out one element in a poem at a time because this makes talking about it easier, but a poem is always more than a mechanical joining together of parts.

While reading these poems, make note of your responses to them. Sometimes isolating and talking about parts of a poem, like sound, can help you explain or understand your particular responses.

Poems
to read and discuss

"OUT, OUT—"

The buzz saw snarled and rattled in the yard
And made dust and dropped stove-length sticks of wood,
Sweet-scented stuff when the breeze drew across it.
And from there those that lifted eyes could count
Five mountain ranges one behind the other
Under the sunset far into Vermont.
And the saw snarled and rattled, snarled and rattled,
As it ran light, or had to bear a load.
And nothing happened: day was all but done.
Call it a day, I wish they might have said   10
To please the boy by giving him the half hour
That a boy counts so much when saved from work.
His sister stood beside them in her apron
To tell them "Supper." At the word, the saw,
As if to prove saws knew what supper meant,
Leaped out at the boy's hand, or seemed to leap—
He must have given the hand. However it was,
Neither refused the meeting. But the hand!
The boy's first outcry was a rueful laugh,
As he swung toward them holding up the hand,   20
Half in appeal, but half as if to keep
The life from spilling. Then the boy saw all—
Since he was old enough to know, big boy
Doing a man's work, though a child at heart—
He saw all spoiled. "Don't let him cut my hand off—
The doctor, when he comes. Don't let him, sister!"
So. But the hand was gone already.
The doctor put him in the dark of ether.
He lay and puffed his lips out with his breath.
And then—the watcher at his pulse took fright.   30

No one believed. They listened at his heart.
Little—less—nothing!—and that ended it.
No more to build on there. And they, since they
Were not the one dead, turned to their affairs.

ROBERT FROST

LISTENING

Outside tonight, earth stretches
   tight as canvas over buds of birth
   that nibble, unseen, at a silence
   stitched loosely with insect sounds.

Along the hall doors crouch to conceal
   noises that press blades to their backs.
   We listen while a dustpan eats
   the scattered pieces of a quarrel.

And elsewhere the bees of love are angry
   as voices predict the distant silence   10
   of divorce with words that apologies
   will dilute but never cleanse.

Domesticity rumbles in the walls
   as waterpipes and drains indicate
   that number six has bathed and now seeks
   one-armed love, lost beneath his blankets.

Next door, locked behind a fear of sudden
   thunder, a child draws stick figures
   of his absent parents and then
   with cries tears them to confetti.   20

Farther down the hall coughs reveal
   the aging couple, dry as gourds, for whom
   the spring night has bred a yellow
   sickness that chokes the grass

And makes crickets clatter like rusty saws.
   For them the tinder of birth has smoldered
   and gone out. They only await the blinding
   scrap of sight before the whole dun world fades.

Avidly, we hear this news of other life
  with ears pressed into the flowered paper   30
  of our walls. Camouflaged, itching among petals,
  we pray they will remain unnoticed

As we listen for hints of ways
  to live; but we find that other rooms
  contain no answers—only lives
  as littered and remorseful as our own.

VERN RUTSALA

OCTOBER SCRIMMAGE

Below the office window
players stretch their cleats
over sweatsocks. They wear
promethean shoulderpads
this ancient afternoon, and I
can hear the murmur of their chatter
magnified down classroom brick
from where I crouch
within my cage of glass.
The team they play for   10
is famous in this town, and they
are all heroes. On the field
the scrimmage roars in dust
the wind whirls from the west
away, always from the west
away, and the sun there
wrinkles a shadow line of oak
against the school wall
in back of the boys who spit
on their hands and roll laces   20
to thread impossible eyes.

JOHN KNOEPFLE

I HEARD A FLY BUZZ—WHEN I DIED

I heard a Fly buzz—when I died—
The Stillness in the Room
Was like the Stillness in the Air—
Between the Heaves of Storm—

The Eyes around—had wrung them dry—
And Breaths were gathering firm
For that last Onset—when the King
Be witnessed—in the Room—

I willed my Keepsakes—Signed away
What portion of me be   10
Assignable—and then it was
There interposed a Fly—

With Blue—uncertain stumbling Buzz—
Between the light—and me—
And then the Windows failed—and then
I could not see to see—

EMILY DICKINSON

SILENCE

Silence: one would willingly
Consume it, eat it like bread.
There is never enough. Now,
When we are silent, metal
Still rings upon shuddering
Metal; a door slams; a child
Cries; other lives surround us.

But remember, there is no
Silence within; the belly
Sighs, grumbles, and what is that   10
Loud knocking, that summoning?
A drum beats, a drum beats. Hear
Your own noisy machine, which
Is moving towards silence.

EDWARD LUCIE-SMITH

SONIC BOOM

I'm sitting in the living room,
When, up above, the Thump of Doom
Resounds. Relax. It's sonic boom.

The ceiling shudders at the clap,
The mirrors tilt, the rafters snap,
And Baby wakens from his nap.

"Hush, babe. Some pilot we equip,
Giving the speed of sound the slip,
Has cracked the air like a penny whip."

Our world is far from frightening; I   10
No longer strain to read the sky
Where moving fingers (jet planes) fly.
Our world seems much too tame to die.

And if it does, with one more pop,
I shan't look up to see it drop.

JOHN UPDIKE

THE CURATIVE POWERS OF SILENCE

Suddenly
I touch upon wordlessness,
I who have watched Cheryl
the blind young woman
who lives up the street
out walking at night
when she thinks no one's looking
deliberately heading
into hedges & trees
to touch them & seemingly   10
to also be kissed,
thus are we each
hugged & kissed,
kissed in daylight,
licked in a fog

Wordless
I fill up
listening for nothing
for nothing at all

as when in life (so-   20
called) I am set
shivering with warmth
by a child-like vision
of the Cheryl in me
(when I think no one's looking)
plopped in a field
of feathery grass
under watchful trees
letting the pre-mind dream
of nothing at all   30
nothing at all,
no flicker
no shadow
no voice
no cry,

not even dreaming

—being dreamed

AL YOUNG

A NOISELESS PATIENT SPIDER

A noiseless patient spider,
I mark'd where on a little promontory it stood isolated,
Mark'd how to explore the vacant vast surrounding,
It launch'd forth filament, filament, filament, out of itself,
Ever unreeling them, ever tirelessly speeding them.

And you O my soul where you stand,
Surrounded, detached, in measureless oceans of space,
Ceaselessly musing, venturing, throwing, seeking the spheres
    to connect them,
Till the bridge you will need be form'd, till the ductile anchor
    hold,
Till the gossamer thread you fling catch somewhere, O my
    soul.   10

WALT WHITMAN

TWELFTH SONG OF THE THUNDER

The voice that beautifies the land!
The voice above,
The voice of the thunder.
Within the dark cloud
Again and again it sounds,
The voice that beautifies the land.

The voice that beautifies the land!
The voice below:
The voice of the grasshopper.
Among the plants   10
Again and again it sounds,
The voice that beautifies the land.

      AMERICAN INDIAN, NAVAJO, TRADITIONAL

SONG FOR SAINT CECILIA'S DAY, 1687

From Harmony, from heavenly Harmony
    This universal frame began:
When Nature underneath a heap
    Of jarring atoms lay
  And could not heave her head,
The tuneful voice was heard from high
    Arise, ye more than dead!
Then cold, and hot, and moist, and dry
In order to their stations leap,
    And Music's power obey.   10
From harmony, from heavenly harmony
    This universal frame began:
    From harmony to harmony
Through all the compass of the notes it ran,
The diapason closing full in Man.

What passion cannot Music raise and quell?
    When Jubal struck the chorded shell
  His listening brethren stood around,
    And, wondering, on their faces fell
  To worship that celestial sound.   20
Less than a god they thought there could not dwell
    Within the hollow of that shell
    That spoke so sweetly and so well.
What passion cannot Music raise and quell?

The trumpet's loud clangor
  Excites us to arms,
With shrill notes of anger
  And mortal alarms.
The double double double beat
  Of the thundering drum   30
  Cries, 'Hark! the foes come;
Charge, charge, 'tis too late to retreat!'

The soft complaining flute
  In dying notes discovers
  The woes of hopeless lovers,
Whose dirge is whisper'd by the warbling lute.

Sharp violins proclaim
Their jealous pangs and desperation,
Fury, frantic indignation,
Depth of pains, and height of passion   40
    For the fair disdainful dame.

But oh! what art can teach,
What human voice can reach
    The sacred organ's praise?
Notes inspiring holy love,
    Notes that wing their heavenly ways
To mend the choirs above.

Orpheus could lead the savage race,
And trees unrooted left their place
    Sequacious of the lyre: 50
But bright Cecilia raised the wonder higher:
When to her Organ vocal breath was given,
An Angel heard, and straight appear'd—
    Mistaking Earth for Heaven!

                GRAND CHORUS

    As from the power of sacred lays
        The spheres began to move.
    And sung the great Creator's praise
        To all the blest above;
    So when the last and dreadful hour
    This crumbling pageant shall devour   60
    The trumpet shall be heard on high
    The dead shall live, the living die
    And Music shall untune the sky

                            JOHN DRYDEN

THE CONSUMER

My eyes catch and stick
as I wade in bellysoft heat.
Tree of miniature chocolates filled with liqueurs,
tree of earrings tinkling in the mink wind,

of Bach oratorios spinning light at 33 1/3,
tree of Thailand silks murmuring changes.
Pluck, eat and grow heavy.
Choose and buy: your taste defines you.
From each hair a wine bottle dangles.
A toaster is strung through my nose.   10
An elevator is installed in my spine.
The mouth of the empire
eats onward through the apple of all.
Armies of brown men
are roasted into coffee beans,
are melted into chocolate,
are pounded into copper.
Their blood is refined into oil,
black river oozing rainbows
of affluence.   20
Their bodies shrink
to grains of rice.
I have lost my knees.
I am the soft mouth of the caterpillar
Men and landscapes are my food
and I grow fat and blind.

                                MARGE PIERCY

DURING WIND AND RAIN

   They sing their dearest songs—
   He, she, all of them—yea,
   Treble and tenor and bass,
        And one to play;
   With the candles mooning each face. . . .
        Ah, no; the years O!
How the sick leaves reel down in throngs!

   They clear the creeping moss—
   Elders and juniors—aye,
   Making the pathways neat   10
        And the garden gay;
   And they build a shady seat. . . .
        Ah, no; the years, the years;
See, the white storm-birds wing across!

They are blithely breakfasting all—
Men and maidens—yea,
Under the summer tree,
  With a glimpse of the bay,
While pet fowl come to the knee. . . .
    Ah, no; the years O!   20
And the rotten rose is ript from the wall.

They change to a high new house,
He, she, all of them—aye,
Clocks and carpets and chairs
  On the lawn all day,
And brightest things that are theirs. . . .
    Ah, no; the years, the years;
Down their carved names the rain-drop ploughs.

THOMAS HARDY

LONDON

I wander thro' each charter'd street,
Near where the charter'd Thames does flow,
And mark in every face I meet
Marks of weakness, marks of woe.

In every cry of every Man,
In every Infant's cry of fear,
In every voice, in every ban,
The mind-forg'd manacles I hear.

How the Chimney-sweeper's cry
Every black'ning Church appalls;   10
And the hapless Soldier's sigh
Runs in blood down Palace walls.

But most thro' midnight streets I hear
How the youthful Harlot's curse
Blasts the new born Infant's tear,
And blights with plagues the Marriage hearse.

WILLIAM BLAKE

AWARD

A Gold Watch to the FBI
Man who has followed
me for 25 years.

Well, old spy
looks like I
led you down some pretty blind alleys,
took you on several trips to Mexico,
fishing in the high Sierras,
jazz at the Philharmonic.
You've watched me all your life,
I've clothed your wife,
put your two sons through college.
what good has it done?   10
the sun keeps rising every morning.
ever see me buy an Assistant President?
or close a school?
or lend money to Trujillo?
ever catch me rigging airplane prices?
I bought some after-hours whiskey in L.A.
but the Chief got his pay.
I ain't killed no Koreans
or fourteen-year-old boys in Mississippi.
neither did I bomb Guatemala,   20
or lend guns to shoot Algerians.
I admit I took a Negro child
to a white rest room in Texas,
but she was my daughter, only three,
who had to pee.

                                        RAY DUREM

KUBLA KHAN

In Xanadu did Kubla Khan
A stately pleasure-dome decree:
Where Alph, the sacred river, ran
Through caverns measureless to man
    Down to a sunless sea.

So twice five miles of fertile ground
With walls and towers were girdled round:
And there were gardens bright with sinuous rills,
Where blossomed many an incense-bearing tree;
And here were forests ancient as the hills,   10
Enfolding sunny spots of greenery.

But oh! that deep romantic chasm which slanted
Down the green hill athwart a cedarn cover!
A savage place! as holy and enchanted
As e'er beneath a waning moon was haunted
By woman wailing for her demon-lover!
And from this chasm, with ceaseless turmoil seething,
As if this earth in fast thick pants were breathing,
A mighty fountain momently was forced:
Amid whose swift half-intermitted burst   20
Huge fragments vaulted like rebounding hail,
Or chaffy grain beneath the thresher's flail:
And 'mid these dancing rocks at once and ever
It flung up momently the sacred river.
Five miles meandering with a mazy motion
Through wood and dale the sacred river ran,
Then reached the caverns measureless to man,
And sank in tumult to a lifeless ocean:
And 'mid this tumult Kubla heard from far
Ancestral voices prophesying war!   30
    The shadow of the dome of pleasure
    Floated midway on the waves;
    Where was heard the mingled measure
    From the fountain and the caves.
It was a miracle of rare device,
A sunny pleasure-dome with caves of ice!

    A damsel with a dulcimer
    In a vision once I saw:
    It was an Abyssinian maid,
    And on her dulcimer she played,   40
    Singing of Mount Abora.
    Could I revive within me
    Her symphony and song,
    To such a deep delight 'twould win me,
That with music loud and long,
I would build that dome in air,
That sunny dome! those caves of ice!

And all who heard should see them there,
And all should cry, Beware! Beware!
His flashing eyes, his floating hair!   50
Weave a circle round him thrice,
And close your eyes with holy dread,
For he on honey-dew hath fed,
And drunk the milk of Paradise.

SAMUEL TAYLOR COLERIDGE

YOU ARE THE BRAVE

You are the brave who do not break
In the grip of the mob when the blow comes straight
To the shattered bone; when the sockets shriek;
When your arms lie twisted under your back.

Good men holding their courage slack
In their frightened pockets see how weak
The work that is done; and feel the weight
Of your blood on the ground for their spirit's sake;

And build their anger, stone on stone;
Each silently, but not alone.

RAY PATTERSON

ARMS AND THE BOY

Let the boy try along this bayonet-blade
How cold steel is, and keen with hunger of blood;
Blue with all malice, like a madman's flash;
And thinly drawn with famishing for flesh.

Lend him to stroke these blind, blunt bullet-heads
Which long to nuzzle in the hearts of lads,
Or give him cartridges of fine zinc teeth,
Sharp with the sharpness of grief and death.

For his teeth seem for laughing round an apple.
There lurk no claws behind his fingers supple;   10
And God will grow no talons at his heels,
Nor antlers through the thickness of his curls.

WILFRED OWEN

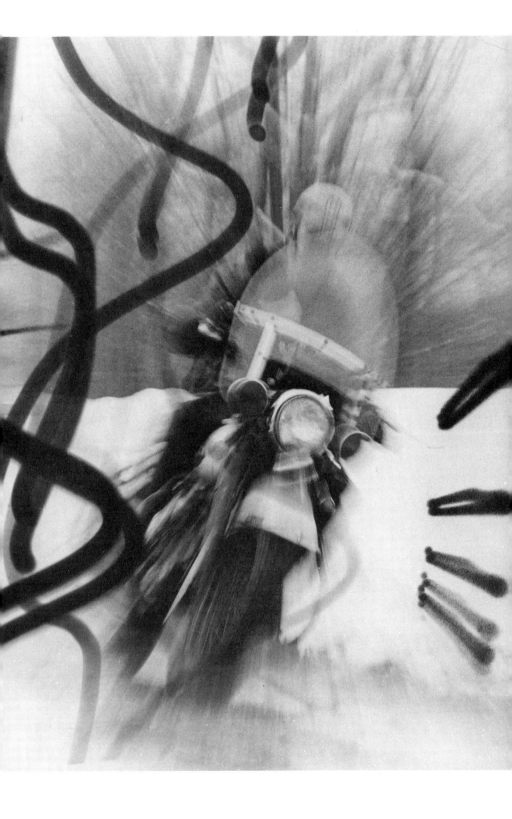

MY PAPA'S WALTZ

The whiskey on your breath
Could make a small boy dizzy;
But I hung on like death:
Such waltzing was not easy.

We romped until the pans
Slid from the kitchen shelf;
My mother's countenance
Could not unfrown itself.

The hand that held my wrist
Was battered on one knuckle;   10
At every step you missed
My right ear scraped a buckle.

You beat time on my head
With a palm caked hard by dirt,
Then waltzed me off to bed
Still clinging to your shirt.

                    THEODORE ROETHKE

PROTHALAMION

Calm was the day, and through the trembling air
    Sweet-breathing Zephyrus did softly play—
    A gentle spirit, that lightly did delay
Hot Titan's beams, which then did glister fair;
        When I (whom sullen care,
Through discontent of my long fruitless stay
    In princes' court, and expectation vain
Of idle hopes, which still do fly away
    Like empty shadows, did afflict my brain)
        Walk'd forth to ease my pain   10
Along the shore of silver-streaming Thames;
Whose rutty bank, the which his river hems,
    Was painted all with variable flowers,
And all the meads adorn'd with dainty gems
        Fit to deck maidens' bowers,
        And crown their paramours
Against the bridal day, which is not long:
Sweet Thames! run softly, till I end my song.

There in a meadow by the river's side
  A flock of nymphs I chancéd to espy,   20
  All lovely daughters of the flood thereby,
With goodly greenish locks all loose untied
    As each had been a bride;
And each one had a little wicker basket
  Made of fine twigs, entrailéd curiously,
In which they gather'd flowers to fill their flasket,
And with fine fingers cropt full feateously
    The tender stalks on high.
Of every sort which in that meadow grew
They gather'd some; the violet, pallid blue,   30
  The little daisy that at evening closes,
The virgin lily and the primrose true,
    With store of vermeil roses,
    To deck their bridegrooms' posies
Against the bridal day, which was not long:
Sweet Thames! run softly, till I end my song.

With that I saw two swans of goodly hue
  Come softly swimming down along the lee;
  Two fairer birds I yet did never see;
The snow which doth the top of Pindus strow   40
    Did never whiter show,
Nor Jove himself, when he a swan would be
  For love of Leda, whiter did appear;
Yet Leda was (they say) as white as he,
  Yet not so white as these, nor nothing near;
    So purely white they were,
That even the gentle stream, the which them bare,
Seem'd foul to them, and bade his billows spare
  To wet their silken feathers, lest they might
Soil their fair plumes with water not so fair,   50
    And mar their beauties bright,
    That shone as Heaven's light
Against their bridal day, which was not long:
Sweet Thames! run softly, till I end my song.

Eftsoons the nymphs, which now had flowers their fill,
  Ran all in haste to see that silver brood
  As they came floating on the crystal flood;
Whom when they saw, they stood amazéd still
    Their wondering eyes to fill:
Them seem'd they never saw a sight so fair   60

Of fowls, so lovely, that they sure did deem
Them heavenly born, or to be that same pair
  Which through the sky draw Venus' silver team;
    For sure they did not seem
To be begot of any earthly seed,
But rather angels, or of angels' breed;
  Yet were they bred of summer's heat, they say,
In sweetest season, when each flower and weed
    The earth did fresh array;
      So fresh they seem'd as day,   70
Even as their bridal day, which was not long:
Sweet Thames! run softly, till I end my song.

Then forth they all out of their baskets drew
  Great store of flowers, the honour of the field,
  That to the sense did fragrant odours yield,
All which upon those goodly birds they threw
    And all the waves did strew,
That like old Peneus' waters they did seem
  When down along by pleasant Tempe's shore
Scatter'd with flowers, through Thessaly they stream,   80
  That they appear, through lilies' plenteous store,
    Like a bride's chamber-floor.
Two of those nymphs meanwhile two garlands bound
Of freshest flowers which in that mead they found,
  The which presenting all in trim array,
Their snowy foreheads therewithal they crown'd;
    Whilst one did sing this lay
    Prepared against that day,
Against their bridal day, which was not long:
Sweet Thames! run softly, till I end my song.   90

'Ye gentle birds! the world's fair ornament,
  And Heaven's glory, whom this happy hour
  Doth lead unto your lovers' blissful bower,
Joy may you have, and gentle heart's content
    Of your love's couplement;
And let fair Venus, that is queen of love,
  With her heart-quelling son upon you smile,
Whose smile, they say, hath virtue to remove
  All love's dislike, and friendship's faulty guile
    For ever to assoil.   100
Let endless peace your steadfast hearts accord,
And blessed plenty wait upon your board;

And let your bed with pleasures chaste abound,
That fruitful issue may to you afford
 Which may your foes confound,
 And make your joys redound
Upon your bridal day, which is not long:
Sweet Thames! run softly, till I end my song.'

So ended she; and all the rest around
 To her redoubled that her undersong,
 Which said their bridal day should not be long: 110
And gentle Echo from the neighbour ground
 Their accents did resound.
So forth those joyous birds did pass along
 Adown the lee that to them murmur'd low,
As he would speak but that he lack'd a tongue,
 Yet did by signs his glad affection show,
 Making his stream run slow.
And all the fowl which in his flood did dwell
'Gan flock about these twain, that did excel
 The rest, so far as Cynthia doth shend 120
The lesser stars. So they, enrangéd well,
 Did on those two attend,
 And their best service lend
Against their wedding day, which was not long:
Sweet Thames! run softly, till I end my song.

At length they all to merry London came,
 To merry London, my most kindly nurse,
 That to me gave this life's first native source,
Though from another place I take my name, 130
 An house of ancient fame:
There when they came whereas those bricky towers
 The which on Thames' broad aged back do ride,
Where now the studious lawyers have their bowers,
 There whilome wont the Templar-knights to bide,
 Till they decay'd through pride;
Next whereunto there stands a stately place,
Where oft I gainéd gifts and goodly grace
 Of that great lord, which therein wont to dwell,
Whose want too well now feels my friendless case; 140
 But ah! here fits not well
 Old woes, but joys, to tell
Against the bridal day, which is not long:
Sweet Thames! run softly, till I end my song.

Yet therein now doth lodge a noble peer,
   Great England's glory and the world's wide wonder,
   Whose dreadful name late through all Spain did thunder,
And Hercules' two pillars standing near
     Did make to quake and fear:
Fair branch of honour, flower of chivalry!   150
   That fillest England with thy triumphs' fame,
Joy have thou of thy noble victory,
   And endless happiness of thine own name
     That promiseth the same;
That through thy prowess and victorious arms
Thy country may be freed from foreign harms,
   And great Eliza's glorious name may ring
Through all the world, fill'd with thy wide alarms,
     Which some brave Muse may sing
     To ages following,   160
Upon the bridal day, which is not long:
Sweet Thames! run softly, till I end my song.

From those high towers this noble lord issúing
   Like radiant Hesper, when his golden hair
   In th' ocean billows he hath bathéd fair,
Descended to the river's open viewing
     With a great train ensuing.
Above the rest were goodly to be seen
   Two gentle knights of lovely face and feature,
Beseeming well the bower of any queen,   170
   With gifts of wit and ornaments of nature,
     Fit for so goodly stature,
That like the twins of Jove they seem'd in sight
Which deck the baldric of the Heavens bright;
   They two, forth pacing to the river's side,
Received those two fair brides, their love's delight;
     Which, at th' appointed tide,
     Each one did make his bride
Against their bridal day, which is not long:
Sweet Thames! run softly, till I end my song.

                     EDMUND SPENSER

3
Rhythms

Rhythm is another way in which a poem is heard. You need only to listen to music and find yourself tapping your foot or wanting to dance in order to realize how easily you respond to rhythm.

Not only does rhythm have the power to move us physically, but it also has the power to move and influence our emotions and our understanding. To grasp what sort of power rhythm has, think of blues, soul, and hard rock and how their rhythms influence our enjoyment and understanding of the music. Imagine what would happen if a piece you know and like were either sung or played to a lilting 3/4 waltz time. The gay, light quality of the waltz rhythm would contradict and destroy the spirit of these other kinds of music.

Of course rhythm is not only found in music—speech is also rhythmical. Words, phrases, sentences, all have varying rhythms, and, as in music, rhythm in speech also conveys meaning. For instance, a person expresses his anger, excitement, or sadness not only with words but also with the rhythms of speech. Notice how you *necessarily* change the way you say the sentence, "I want to go home," when you use it to express unhappiness, then anger, then excitement.

Like other sound patterns, rhythm strongly appeals to children. Remember nursery rhymes or jumping-rope rhymes? The latter, invented by children themselves, are also good examples of children's lively sense of humor.

> Cinderella—
> Dressed in yellow—
> Went upstairs to kiss a fellow—
> Made a mistake—
> Kissed a snake—
> How many doctors will it take?

It would be almost impossible to read this example of children's verse without the heavy regular beats that accompany the turns of the jump rope.

Poets take advantage of the rhythms naturally present in ordinary speech and manipulate them carefully to communicate the moods, feelings, and attitudes that are as much a part of a poem as the dictionary meanings of the words used. A great many contemporary poets, especially when they abandon formal patterns of rhythm, make use of the rhymths of ordinary speech instead.

LAMENT FOR A BROTHER

So senseless the way it went down,
      as they say.
The day before, carefree, doing
his thing,
      as they say
New day, still carefree but, so
      they say,
BLEW HIS MIND: so they say.
So senseless the way it went down,
playing a game that, as they say,   10
BLEW HIS MIND, so they say.
Never-the-less it's done and
Doing my thing aint no mo' fun now.
Hurt, bitter, angry, confused, and
Alone.
Things just ain't the same
      as they say.

PATRICIA WATSON

In this poem, Patricia Watson adjusts or changes the rhythm of the lines to suggest that the situation is far more serious than the thoughtless contemporary slang phrases are able to express. Conventional expressions, such as "it went down" and "doing his thing," rattled off as they commonly are, seem to take on increasing force as the poem progresses, when the reader is made to pause and repeat the qualifying phrases "as they say" and "so they say" six times. The spacing and capitalization of "BLEW HIS MIND" require a slow, heavy emphasis on each of the three words, shifting the overtones of this slang phrase toward something more ominous than its usual range of implications. This rhythmic arrangement continues to tighten the mood in the last lines, where Patricia Watson ironically balances the deliberately clichéd and quick-paced line, "Doing my thing aint no mo' fun now" against the slow, emphatic, "Hurt, bitter, angry, confused, and / Alone."

Patricia Watson's shifting and irregular rhythms are characteristic of much contemporary poetry. The use of these rhythms implies a rejection of the regular, heavily accented poetry that most students might most readily associate with writers like Edgar Allen Poe, for example, as in the opening lines of his poem "The Sleeper":

> At midnight, in the month of June
> I stand beneath the mystic moon,
> An opiate vapor, dewy dim,
> Exhales from out her golden rim.

The reader almost becomes the sleeper under the influence of this rhythm. These lines serve to carry the reader along in a dreamy half-consciousness. Their rhythms bypass communication rather than assist it, so that the reader doesn't think to ask himself if he knows exactly what the poet is talking about.

Response 10

In a natural way, read the following three poems aloud. Don't force a mechanical or "poetical" rhythm.

ASSASSINATION

It's Hunt's catsup
splattered over the country
like in some movie
and the dead guy
shifted ever so slightly
when a rock fell too close
   but it is real—

this dead man
twitches in our minds
and
we stop to scratch.   10

     PATRICIA PARKER

THE DREAM IN THE CITY

And so I send a letter. Uncollected,
It returns. I try the telephone.
Somebody says, "That number's disconnected."
(How could they go, and leave me here alone?)

Sometimes I turn a corner and before me
Empty in Sunday silence the long views.
A voice calls out, but not to reassure me.
Then I diminish up the avenues.

JOHN N. MORRIS

THE WORLD IS TOO MUCH WITH US

The world is too much with us; late and soon,
Getting and spending, we lay waste our powers:
Little we see in Nature that is ours;
We have given our hearts away, a sordid boon!
This Sea that bares her bosom to the moon,
The winds that will be howling at all hours
And are up-gather'd now like sleeping flowers,
For this, for everything, we are out of tune;
It moves us not.—Great God! I'd rather be
A Pagan suckled in a creed outworn,   10
So might I, standing on this pleasant lea,
Have glimpses that would make me less forlorn;
Have sight of Proteus rising from the sea;
Or hear old Triton blow his wreathéd horn.

WILLIAM WORDSWORTH

Make a note of your reactions to the rhythms of each poem. Do the
rhythms of some lines seem to add to their meaning for you? Don't be
afraid to record negative as well as positive reactions.

_____

Most poets' interest in rhythm is a part of their interest in meaning.
The next poem shows how a poet can adjust the rhythm of his lines to
reinforce the poem's meaning and complement its subject matter.

WHO'S WHO

A shilling life will give you all the facts:
How Father beat him, how he ran away,
What were the struggles of his youth, what acts
Made him the greatest figure of his day:
Of how he fought, fished, hunted, worked all night,
Though giddy, climbed new mountains; named a sea:
Some of the last researchers even write
Love made him weep his pints like you and me.

With all his honours on, he sighed for one
Who, say astonished critics, lived at home;   10
Did little jobs about the house with skill
And nothing else; could whistle; would sit still
Or potter round the garden; answered some
Of his long marvellous letters but kept none.

                            W. H. AUDEN

The lines describing the subject's public career begin brusquely, in the language of a biographical summary. The realization that this is a poem and not a prose paragraph is deliberately delayed. The sequence "fought, fished, hunted, worked all night" has a staccato beat that both suggests the restless energy of the man and echoes the no-nonsense prose rhythms with which the poem opens. The first five lines are rapid. Beginning with "climbed new mountains, named a sea" the fuller vowel sounds force a slower pace that flows transitionally into the longest phrase of the first part of the poem, "Some of the last researchers even write / Love made him weep his pints like you and me." These lines prepare the reader for the quieter mood and rhythms of the next stanza, where the phrases move slowly from one line into the next. Instead of the commas which predominate in the first stanza, semicolons, which signal longer pauses, separate the phrases, slow the pace, and create a rhythm paralleling the satisfying, slow-moving life that the lines describe.

The following poem also represents a change in feeling through a change in rhythm.

HOW SHE RESOLVED TO ACT

"I shall be careful to say nothing at all
About myself or what I know of him
Or the vaguest thought I have—no matter how dim,
Tonight if it so happen that he call."

And not ten minutes later the doorbell rang
And into the hall he stepped as he always did
With a face and a bearing that quite poorly hid
His brain that burned and his heart that fairly sang
And his tongue that wanted to be rid of the truth.

As well as she could, for she was very loath   10
To signify how she felt, she kept very still,
But soon her heart cracked loud as a coffee mill
And her brain swung like a comet in the dark
And her tongue raced like a squirrel in the park.

MERRILL MOORE

There is a tension between how the young woman plans to behave and how she finally does, despite her strong resolution. The first stanza is full of stops and starts, of qualifications that mirror her thought process as she resolves to be cool and proper when her expected visitor arrives. Once she has made up her mind, her determination becomes firm as she pauses to draw a deep breath before saying "no matter how dim." When the visitor arrives, however, the lines suddenly move quickly, with no commas, dashes, or verbal qualifications to slow the reader down. Their speed communicates the excitement of the moment and the girl's response to the eagerness of her visitor. The rhythm of the final stanza parallels the shifting feelings of the girl. In the first two lines, she tries to hold herself back, keeping to her resolution—"As well as she could, for she was very loath/To signify how she felt, she kept very still"—and the pauses at the ends and in the middle of each line keep pace with her internal struggle. When she is unsuccessful, however, and gives in to her emotions, the remaining three lines move as fast as her tongue—no pauses, just a continuous stream of words in unqualified phrases. Finally she dares to communicate her feelings freely.

Response 11

You have seen how W. H. Auden in "Who's Who" and Merrill Moore in "How She Resolved to Act" led the reader to sense a change in mood through rhythm. Write a poem, no longer than the last two examples, in which you change its mood by altering its rhythm, just as Auden and Moore did in the last stanzas of their poems. The subject can be of your own choosing, but perhaps you would like to write a poem about an event in which you have experienced some sort of change.

Obviously, the content of a poem influences our responses to its rhythms, but we needn't assume on that account that our responses are purely "in the head." Many rhythms can be technically, even if not perfectly, measured. When we speak of the meters of poetry we are doing something similar to dividing a piece of music into beats, identifying the stressed and unstressed syllables in the lines of a poem and the patterns they make.

Take a word like "running," which breaks into two syllables, unequally stressed. Unless you are very unusual, you will find that when you say the word aloud you stress the first syllable more heavily than the second. Traditionally, critics and students of poetry mark the stronger syllable with a stress mark (ˊ) and the weaker one with a slack (˘). But this practice is obviously inadequate to describe a word with more than two syllables—"apartment," for example. Again there is a variation in stress: the strongest syllable is the second and the weakest is the first, but a system that marks only two degrees of stress can only deal very roughly and arbitrarily with the third, relegating it to the category of weak stress. This complication has aroused a good deal of disagreement and discussion among critics and linguists, so that now many of them use a four-stress system for marking degrees of emphasis.

While the conventional meters of English poetry are still marked, as they always have been, according to the two-stress system, poets of course have always been aware of the more varied degrees of emphasis available to them. Conventionally, a repeated two-syllable pattern emphasizing the second syllable (for example, the word "tŏdáy") is called iambic (˘ˊ), while the reverse (for example, "állĕy") is called trochaic (ˊ˘). The three-syllable unit illustrated by a word like "whíspĕrĭng"—an emphasized initial syllable followed by two weaker ones— is called dactylic (ˊ˘˘), while the opposite (not common in English words, but frequent in phrases like "ĭñ thĕ hoúse") is anapestic (˘˘ˊ). It is an open question how useful these terms are to the student; certainly to the poet it is the rhythmic phenomena described, not their names, that matter—and they matter, of course, not as separate units (the units are conventionally called "feet") but in combination. A line of poetry may, theoretically, have any number of such feet, though few will have only one, like the familiar poem on fleas, "Adam / had 'em." Examples with more than five feet will be almost equally rare, though six- and seven-foot lines are familiar to most students of the history of poetry. Most commonly known to the average reader are the four- and five-foot lines (which you will sometimes see called tetrameter and pentameter), which seem to fit in easily with the sound structure of English prose sentences. Beyond these technical matters, most poets have always been aware that, as Ralph Waldo Emerson put it, "it is not meter but a meter-making argument that makes a poem." Poets use and vary the traditional meters to create specific effects.

TO AN ATHLETE DYING YOUNG

The time you won your town the race
We chaired you through the market-place;
Man and boy stood cheering by,
And home we brought you shoulder-high.

To-day, the road all runners come,
Shoulder-high we bring you home,
And set you at your threshold down,
Townsman of a stiller town.

Smart lad, to slip betimes away
From fields where glory does not stay,   10
And early though the laurel grows
It withers quicker than the rose.

Eyes the shady night has shut
Cannot see the record cut,
And silence sounds no worse than cheers
After earth has stopped the ears.

Now you will not swell the rout
Of lads that wore their honours out,
Runners whom renown outran
And the name died before the man.   20

So set, before its echoes fade,
The fleet foot on the sill of shade,
And hold to the low lintel up
The still-defended challenge-cup.

And round that early-laurelled head
Will flock to gaze the strengthless dead,
And find unwithered on its curls
The garland briefer than a girl's.

                    A. E. HOUSMAN

ℛesponse 12

See if you can pick out the metrical pattern of "To an Athlete Dying
Young." First divide the words in the poem's first two stanzas into
syllables, then read the poem in a normal voice and mark each syllable
with either a stress or a slack. What pattern seems to be repeated, and
how frequently? The pattern you discover won't be perfectly regular,
but, in spite of disagreement on the marking of a few syllables, most

readers will find the same underlying metrical order. That order provides a framework in which exceptions can meaningfully occur. When you discover such exceptions, circle them and ask yourself why Housman chose to contradict the regular meter.

Here are some conclusions you may have drawn from your observations of Housman's use of meter. With perhaps the exception of the third line, the meter of the first stanza of the poem—the pattern we call iambic tetrameter—is regular. As a result, the reader is almost hypnotized, lulled by the poem's repeated metrical beat. He gets used to hearing the recurring ∪⁄. When the second stanza begins, the regular, lulling rhythm begins again. Suddenly, in the second line, the reader feels a jolt; his expectations of a continued regular beat are not met. The line begins with a strong syllable, a stress, rather than a slack— "shoúlder-high." The reader feels this stress again in the final line of the second stanza, "Tównsman of a stiller town." Why has Housman given the reader such a jolt? What is to be gained? Obviously, he wants him to sit up and pay attention to the lines, but he also wants him to notice that the athlete's strong, healthy, and apparently promising life has been reversed—like the meter—and turned into death. Once the townspeople had held the athlete "shoulder-high" in victory, but now that he is dead it is his coffin that they carry "shoulder-high." Housman manipulates the poem's meter to make the reader feel the full shock value of the athlete's death.

For another example of how iambic tetrameter can be more than just routine, look at the poem below.

DELIGHT IN DISORDER

A sweet disorder in the dress
Kindles in clothes a wantonness:—
A lawn about the shoulders thrown
Into a fine distractión,—
An erring lace, which here and there
Enthrals the crimson stomacher—
A cuff neglectful, and thereby
Ribbands to flow confusedly,—
A winning wave, deserving note,
In the tempestuous petticoat,—   10

A careless shoe-string, in whose tie
I see a wild civility,—
Do more bewitch me, than when art
Is too precise in every part.

ROBERT HERRICK

Once again the pattern is not completely regular. Why has Herrick pur-
posely varied the pattern and knocked the reader off balance in practi-
cally every other line? The answer lies in the poet's subject matter. Her-
rick looks at a woman from head to foot and discovers that he likes the
disorder of her clothing better than he would if it were perfectly neat
and tidy. To share this delight with the reader, he varies the poem's
meter so that it is pleasantly disordered like the woman's appearance. A
meter "too precise in every part" would be, like such a woman, chilling.

Pauses, sometimes at the ends of lines and sometimes even more
effectively within them, are important in traditional metrical poetry. In
William Wordsworth's "Sonnet Composed upon Westminster Bridge"
the speaker experiences a revelation. Early in the morning he looks at
the sleeping city of London and realizes that it is like a living, breathing
being. Wordsworth communicates the importance he attaches to this
new awareness partly by making his reader pause—in the next-to-the-
last line—after the exclamation "Dear God!"

SONNET COMPOSED UPON WESTMINSTER BRIDGE

Earth has not anything to show more fair:
Dull would he be of soul who could pass by
A sight so touching in its majesty:
This City now doth like a garment wear
The beauty of the morning: silent, bare,
Ships, towers, domes, theatres, and temples lie
Open unto the fields, and to the sky,
All bright and glittering in the smokeless air.
Never did sun more beautifully steep
In his first splendour valley, rock, or hill;   10
Ne'er saw I, never felt, a calm so deep!
The river glideth at his own sweet will:
Dear God! the very houses seem asleep;
And all that mighty heart is lying still!

WILLIAM WORDSWORTH

Response 13

TRIAD

These be
Three silent things:
The falling snow . . . the hour
Before the dawn . . . the mouth of one
Just dead.

ADELAIDE CRAPSEY

Locate the pauses in this poem and decide how they help, along with the three things actually named, to create the mood of the poem. Now think of three more silent things from your own experience, consider what mood they might suggest, and try to arrange them in a short poem whose pauses reinforce your meaning. See if others in the class respond to what you have tried to express without your naming it.

Poems
to read and discuss

AUGUST 24, 1963—1:00 A.M.—OMAHA

Heavy breathing fills all my chamber
Sinister Trucks prowl
      down dim-lit alleyways.
Racing past each other,
      cars toot obscenities.
Silence is crawling in open windows
      smiling and warm.
Suddenly,
      crickets and cockroaches
      join in the madness: 10
      cricking and crawling.
Here I am!
A portion of some murky design.
Writing,
      because I cannot sleep,
      because I could die here.

           DONNA WHITEWING

NIGHT JOURNEY

Now as the train bears west,
Its rhythm rocks the earth,
And from my Pullman berth
I stare into the night
While others take their rest.

Bridges of iron lace,
A suddenness of trees,
A lap of mountain mist
All cross my line of sight,
Then a bleak wasted place,   10
And a lake below my knees.
Full on my neck I feel
The straining at a curve;
My muscles move with steel,
I wake in every nerve.
I watch a beacon swing
From dark to blazing bright;
We thunder through ravines
And gullies washed with light.
Beyond the mountain pass   20
Mist deepens on the pane;
We rush into a rain
That rattles double glass.
Wheels shake the roadbed stone,
The pistons jerk and shove,
I stay up half the night
To see the land I love.

       THEODORE ROETHKE

PREFACE TO A TWENTY VOLUME SUICIDE NOTE

Lately, I've become accustomed to the way
The ground opens up and envelops me
Each time I go out to walk the dog.
Or the broad edged silly music the wind
Makes when I run for a bus—

Things have come to that.

And now, each night I count the stars,
And each night I get the same number.
And when they will not come to be counted
I count the holes they leave.   10

Nobody sings anymore.

And then last night, I tiptoed up
To my daughter's room and heard her
Talking to someone, and when I opened
The door, there was no one there . . .
Only she on her knees,
Peeking into her own clasped hands.

LEROI JONES

A SATIRICAL ELEGY ON THE DEATH OF A LATE FAMOUS GENERAL

His Grace! impossible! what dead!
Of old age too, and in his bed!
And could that Mighty Warrior fall?
And so inglorious, after all!
Well, since he's gone, no matter how,
The last loud trump must wake him now:
And, trust me, as the noise grows stronger,
He'd wish to sleep a little longer.
And could he be indeed so old
As by the news-papers we're told?   10
Threescore, I think, is pretty high;
'Twas time in conscience he should die.
This world he cumber'd long enough;
He burnt his candle to the snuff;
And that's the reason, some folks think,
He left behind *so great a stink.*
Behold his funeral appears,
Nor widow's sighs, nor orphan's tears,
Wont at such times each heart to pierce,
Attend the progress of his hearse.   20
But what of that, his friends may say,
He had those honours in his day.
True to his profit and his pride,
He made them weep before he dy'd.

    Come hither, all ye empty things,
Ye bubbles rais'd by breath of Kings;
Who float upon the tide of state,
Come hither, and behold your fate.

Let pride be taught by this rebuke,
How very mean a thing's a Duke;   30
From all his ill-got honours flung,
Turn'd to that dirt from whence he sprung.

JONATHAN SWIFT

from SONGS OF INNOCENCE

Nurse's Song

When the voices of children are heard on the green
And laughing is heard on the hill,
My heart is at rest within my breast
   And everything else is still.

"Then come home, my children, the sun is gone down
And the dews of night arise;
Come, come, leave off play, and let us away
Till the morning appears in the skies."

"No, no, let us play, for it is yet day
And we cannot go to sleep;   10
Besides, in the sky the little birds fly
And the hills are all cover'd with sheep."

"Well, well, go & play till the light fades away
And then go home to bed."
The little ones leaped & shouted & laugh'd
   And all the hills ecchoéd.

WILLIAM BLAKE

from SONGS OF EXPERIENCE

Nurse's Song

When the voices of children are heard on the green
And whisp'rings are in the dale,
The days of my youth rise fresh in my mind,
My face turns green and pale.

Then come home, my children, the sun is gone down,
And the dews of night arise;
Your spring & your day are wasted in play,
And your winter and night in disguise.

WILLIAM BLAKE

GOING UPTOWN TO VISIT MIRIAM

on the train
old ladies playing football
going for empty seats

very funny persons

the train riders
                are silly people
                i am a train rider

but no one knows where i am
going to take this train

to take this train   10
to take this train

the ladies   read popular
paperbacks   because they
are popular   they get off
at 42 to change for the
westside line   or off
59 for the department store

the train pulls in & out
the white walls   dark-
ness   white walls   dark-   20
ness

ladies looking up   i
wonder where they going
the dentist   pick up
husband pick up wife
pick up kids

pick up ?grass?
to library   to museum
to laundromat   to school

but no one knows where i am   30
going to take this train

to take this train

to visit miriam
to visit miriam

& to kiss her
on the cheek
& hope i don't
see sonia on the
street

But no one knows where i'm taking   40
this train
        taking this train
        to visit miriam.

        VICTOR HERNANDEZ CRUZ

BUT HE WAS COOL OR: HE EVEN STOPPED FOR GREEN LIGHTS

super-cool
ultrablack
a tan/purple
had a beautiful shade.

he had a double-natural
that wd put the sisters to shame.
his dashikis were tailor made
& his beads were imported sea shells
    (from some blk/country i never heard of)
he was triple-hip.   10

his tikis were hand carved
out of ivory
& came express from the motherland.
he would greet u in swahili
and say good-by in yoruba.
woooooooooooo-jim he bes so cool & ill tel li gent
        cool-cool is so cool he was un-cooled by
                other niggers' cool
        cool-cool ultracool was bop-cool/ice box
                cool so cool cold cool   20
        his wine didn't have to be cooled, him was
                air conditioned cool
        cool-cool/real cool made me cool—now
                ain't that cool
        cool-cool so cool him nick-named refrig-
                erator.

cool-cool so cool
he didn't know,
after detroit, newark, chicago &c.,
we had to hip   30
        cool-cool/ super cool/ real cool
    that
    to be black
    is
    to be
    very-hot.

                        DON L. LEE

FATHER

When father goes to see his only daughter
in the foster home where she is treated well,
hat in hand he stands before the butler
and the foster mother says "O it is that man"—
her eyes descend to search him on the landing
as she whispers warning in his daughter's ear.

JOHN LACHS

FOR THE TRUTH

(because it is necessary)

in the tea rooms
of our revolution
we blatantly debate
our knowledge of world revolts
—our anxious ears only half-listened
to the songs of the martinique
who sings in muffled tones
from beneath a mechanized tombstone
built by the pulp of greedy merchants
who got stoned on the juices of our servitude   10
& who write prefaces to our "negritude"

from the tea rooms
of our revolution we emerge
to pamphleteer
the anticipatory designs
of our dead
& exiled poets
—without sanctions
from our unsuspecting brothers
whose death we so naively plot   20
(we engage in a hypothetical revolt
against a not-so-hypothetical enemy)

what kind of man are you
black revolutionary, so-called?

what kind of man are you trying to be
ultra-hip-revolutionary-nationalist-
quasi-strategist-ego-centric-phony
intellectual romantic black prima donna child
—screaming, "revolution means change . . ."
never finishing the sentence   30
or the thought
talking about "para-military"
strategy and techniques
publicizing a so-called underground program
wearing your military garb
as if you never heard of camouflage
so in love with intrigue
you have no thoughts
about the post-revolution life
that the total destruction   40
you talk about assumes . . .

you leave me quite confused
brother
i don't know who the enemy is
anymore
perhaps it is me, myself, because
i have these thoughts
in the tea rooms of our revolution.

                              EDWARD S. SPRIGGS

AMBITION

This summer I shall
Return to our Longhouse,
Hide beneath a feathered hat,
And become an Old Man.

                              PHIL GEORGE

THE DEEP BREATHER

Taking deep breaths rapidly,
stiffening the stomach muscles—
          black-out . . .

Children learn the process
by accident and make it a rite—
dots before the eyes . . .

the horizon swooping up,
vanishing . . .
and instantly, it seems to the breather,

things righting themselves   10
and he's sitting on the ground
shaking his head

watching the dots melt.
The children who saw
his eyes roll back

and who pinched him cruelly
to no response
always laugh when he returns

and ask him how it was.
The deep breather   20
can never answer

except to stare at the earth
and shake his head, while
smiling a slow, soft smile.

GERALD DUFF

RUNAGATE RUNAGATE

I

Runs falls rises stumbles on from darkness into darkness
and the darkness thicketed with shapes of terror
and the hunters pursuing and the hounds pursuing
and the night cold and the night long and the river
to cross and the jack-muh-lanterns beckoning beckoning
and blackness ahead and when shall I reach that somewhere
morning and keep on going and never turn back and keep on
   going

                Runagate
                        Runagate
                                Runagate   10

Many thousands rise and go
many thousands crossing over
                                    O mythic North
                        O star-shaped yonder Bible city

Some go weeping and some rejoicing
some in coffins and some in carriages
some in silks and some in shackles

            Rise and go or fare you well

No more auction block for me
no more driver's lash for me   20

        If you see my Pompey, 30 yrs of age,
        new breeches, plain stockings, negro shoes;
        if you see my Anna, likely young mulatto
        branded E on the right cheek, R on the left,
        catch them if you can and notify subscriber.
        Catch them if you can, but it won't be easy.
        They'll dart underground when you try to catch them,
        plunge into quicksand, whirlpools, mazes,
        turn into scorpions when you try to catch them.

And before I'll be a slave   30
I'll be buried in my grave

        North star and bonanza gold
        I'm bound for the freedom, freedom-bound
        and oh Susyanna don't you cry for me

                    Runagate

                        Runagate

II

Rises from their anguish and their power,

                    Harriet Tubman,

woman of earth, whipscarred,
a summoning, a shining   40

Mean to be free

And this was the way of it, brethren brethren,
way we journeyed from Can't to Can.
Moon so bright and no place to hide,
the cry up and the patterollers riding,·
hound dogs belling in bladed air.
And fear starts a-murbling, Never make it,
we'll never make it. *Hush that now,*
and she's turned upon us, levelled pistol
glinting in the moonlight: 50
Dead folks can't jaybird-talk, she says;
you keep on going now or die, she says.

Wanted   Harriet Tubman   alias The General
alias Moses   Stealer of Slaves

In league with Garrison   Alcott   Emerson
Garrett   Douglass   Thoreau   John Brown

Armed and known to be Dangerous

Wanted   Reward   Dead or Alive

Tell me, Ezekiel, oh tell me do you see
mailed Jehovah coming to deliver me?   60

Hoot-owl calling in the ghosted air,
five times calling to the hants in the air.
Shadow of a face in the scary leaves,
shadow of a voice in the talking leaves:

Come ride-a my train

Oh that train, ghost-story train
through swamp and savanna movering movering,
over trestles of dew, through caves of the wish,
Midnight Special on a sabre track movering movering,
first stop Mercy and the last Hallelujah.   70

Come ride-a my train

Mean mean mean to be free.

ROBERT HAYDEN

82

4
Details: Sights, Smells, Textures

In the following poem, the poet pauses long enough to see two details most of us would barely stop to notice.

A DAY BEGINS

A headless squirrel, some blood
oozing from the unevenly
chewed-off neck

lies in rainsweet grass
near the woodshed door.
Down the driveway

the first irises
have opened since dawn,
ethereal, their mauve

almost a transparent gray,   10
their dark veins
bruise-blue.

       DENISE LEVERTOV

Most people usually look quickly away from a dead animal, just as they pass by flowers in a hurry, perhaps saying "How pretty!" but certainly not stopping to examine an individual flower. The very fact that Denise Levertov takes time to observe precisely becomes her comment on what she sees: such small details can set the tone of a day and thus can matter more than people might think.

Touching, tasting, seeing, smelling—the poet relies on all these senses, not only upon hearing. These sensations spring from a real world, a world that the poet naturally receives all at once, not with one sense at a time. Everyone shares in and is aware of this world, at least enough to get around in it, but the poet must constantly heighten and refine his awareness, must notice and respond to objects and sensations which people usually pass by or take for granted.

Response 14

Using your own surroundings, focus on *one* detail that seems significant, or mysterious, to you but that you feel other people overlook or fail to appreciate and write a poem that presents your observation to them. The following piece may be used as a model.

I

wonder why
some

people
leave the
front

porch
light still
on

in
the burning
bright

hotness
of summer
day

noontime.

10

    TOM POOLE

By selecting details that stimulate the reader's senses, a poet can involve the reader emotionally in the experience of his poem. Robert Hayden makes the reader feel the poverty and decay of a Mexican street market by presenting to him the smell of its rotting carcasses, the sight of cigarette ashes about to drop onto overripe fruit, and the sound of the crippled beggar crying bitterly for charity while the wealthy tourists "stride" by on "hard good legs." Each line contributes a fragment to the overwhelming rush of sense impressions.

MARKET

Ragged boys
lift sweets, haggle
for acid-green
and bloody gelatins.
A broken smile
dandles its weedy
cigarette
over papayas too ripe
and pyramids
of rotting oranges.   10
Turkeys like feather-
duster flowers
lie trussed in bunchy smother.
The barefoot cripple
foraging crawls
among rinds, orts,
chewed butts, trampled
peony droppings—
his hunger litany
and suppliant before   20
altars of mamey,
pineapple, mango.
Turistas pass.
Por caridad, por caridad.
Lord, how they stride
on the hard good legs
money has made them.

Ay! you creatures
who have walked
on seas of money all   30
your foreign lives!
Por caridad.
Odor of a dripping
carcass moans
beneath the hot
fragrance of carnations,
cool scent of lilies.
Starveling dogs
hover in the reek
of frying; ashy feet   40
(the twistfoot beggar laughs)
kick at them in vain.
Aloft, the Fire King's
flashing mask of tin
looks down with eyes
of sunstruck glass.

ROBERT HAYDEN

Similarly in "Senior Citizens' City," by Randy Dunagan, the "old
People noises," the "coughs, belches, growls, spits," and the repeated

reminder of the emergency button in the bathroom reveal the under-lying terror in a housing complex for the old. These details become more forceful because of the contrast with the "children playing," whom the "senior citizens" never see in their "Fun-Senior-Citizen-close-knit / Communities," just as the beggar and the tourists in Robert Hayden's "Market" make each other's presence more vivid.

SENIOR CITIZENS' CITY

Bodies sleeping,
making old People noises
    coughs, belches, growls, spits.
    In every house
    on every street
    old bodies sleeping
    for it is a senior citizen city
the moon watches the hearses,
    the unseen hearses,
sneaking the dead old bodies out   10
    the toilets have buttons
    to press in case you have a heart attack
on the stool
    so people will come to help
    and they're wondering
How do I know the button in my bathroom
works
Old Friends silently sharing the same
Fear
    care written on their Faces   20
They lie awake coughing
    Listening to the death march of the
Rainy day hearse parade
    wondering who,
    then when and how
For they never see children playing
    to show them it was all worthwhile
They only see buttons in bathrooms
and old eyes that reflect their own Fears
    For that's all that's allowed   30
in Fun-Senior-Citizen-close-knit
    Communities,
        Communities terrorized by an unseen terrorist.

RANDY DUNAGAN

ℛesponse 15

Taking "Market" and "Senior Citizens' City" as models, write a poem that uses varied sense impressions—sights, sounds, smells, textures—to describe a place. Robert Hayden's many details and Randy Dunagan's repeated mention of the ominous button suggest techniques you can use to make your poem effective. You may already have a subject in mind, if not, you might attempt one of the following: a bus or train station, a hospital emergency room, your room at home, the dean's office, or a school cafeteria or other eating place.

One way to begin writing your poem is to make a list of the details that strike you when you are in the place you're writing about, or that come to your mind when you think about it. Choose the ones that you think will most effectively tell your reader how you feel about the place you're describing. Eliminate details that don't belong to the effect you want to make.

Not only a place but such intangible things as the time of day can be made more real through the use of details. Jonathan Swift wrote his poem "A Description of the Morning" in 1709, but it can still bring vividly before us the sights and sounds of early morning in eighteenth-century London, even though such details as the "kennel" (an open channel for all sorts of sewage), an array of noisy street vendors, and the crowd of "duns" (bill collectors) have largely disappeared.

A DESCRIPTION OF THE MORNING

Now hardly here and there a Hackney-Coach
Appearing, show'd the Ruddy Morns Approach.
Now *Betty* from her Masters Bed had flown,
And softly stole to discompose her own.
The Slipshod Prentice from his Masters Door,
Had par'd the Dirt, and Sprinkled round the Floor.
Now *Moll* had whirl'd her Mop with dext'rous Airs,
Prepar'd to Scrub the Entry and the Stairs.
The Youth with Broomy Stumps began to trace
The Kennel-Edge, where Wheels had worn the Place.   10
The Smallcoal-Man was heard with Cadence deep,
'Till drown'd in Shriller Notes of *Chimney-Sweep.*

Duns at his Lordships Gate began to meet,
And Brickdust *Moll* had Scream'd through half a Street.
The Turnkey now his Flock returning sees,
Duly let out a Nights to Steal for Fees.
The watchful Bailiffs take their silent Stands,
And School-Boys lag with Satchels in their Hands.

JONATHAN SWIFT

Another poet, writing more than two hundred years later than Swift, also looked at and listened to a London morning.

MORNING AT THE WINDOW

They are rattling breakfast plates in basement kitchens,
And along the trampled edges of the street
I am aware of the damp souls of housemaids
Sprouting despondently at area gates.

The brown waves of fog toss up to me
Twisted faces from the bottom of the street,
And tear from a passer-by with muddy skirts
An aimless smile that hovers in the air
And vanishes along the level of the roofs.

T. S. ELIOT

The servants Eliot refers to are much less vigorous than Swift's Betty and Moll, but they, too, stamp their mood on the time: their dampness and depression seem hopeless and unchangeable. The fog distorts what is seen, so that a face seems detached from a distance and a smile cut loose from a face. The loneliness seems inescapable.

Still another poet, Eugene McCarthy, presents a recurring time, Saturday, in a similar yet somewhat different way from that in which Swift and Eliot describe a morning. Instead of describing one particular time, he suggests the feeling of a typically American, mid-twentieth-century weekend by generalizing about it through details that both characterize the time itself and imply the speaker's attitude toward it. "Saturday" is an ambiguous "promised land," endlessly approached with expectation, but perhaps never reached.

SATURDAY

Saturday is a whale
It swallows people
for three days
Saturday is the sphinx
It has a locked secret
Saturday is Mona Lisa
Its smile is inscrutable
Saturday is a Castro convertible
It is closed all day
Saturday holds its breath   10
Saturday, if it comes,
could last forever

                    EUGENE McCARTHY

Response 16

Write a poem about a time—a particular day or hour—in which you
characterize your subject by details that appeal to the reader's senses.
Morning in a dormitory, Friday rush hour, and Sunday afternoon are all
possibilities.

Details not only spring from and describe the subject, they also indicate
the poet's attitudes and feelings toward it. Different purposes some-
times require different techniques. Jonathan Swift, T. S. Eliot, and
Eugene McCarthy, while they share the purpose of characterizing a
particular time, go about their work in very different ways. Swift's and
Eliot's details are easily visualized, even when they are ironically or
fantastically stated—we can imagine the maid leaving her master, or
the fog as seeming to detach faces from bodies—but McCarthy's
details cannot be visualized—Saturday is a day, not a whale, or the
sphinx, or Mona Lisa, or a convertible sofa. These objects, however,
help McCarthy to express his feelings. "Saturday" stands for every-
one's expectation that the weekend will bring something unique.

The option of calling Saturday a whale or a Castro convertible
enlarges the range from which poets can draw their material and the
uses they can make of it. Another poem by Eugene McCarthy also
uses this option when it makes a child's bicycle ride stand for her
adventurous entrance into the adult world.

BICYCLE RIDER

(to Mary)

Teeth bare to the wind
Knuckle white grip on handle bars
You push the pedals of no return,
Let loose new motion and speed.
The earth turns with the multiplied
Force of your wheels.
Do not look back.
Feet light on the brake
Ride the bicycle of your will
Down the spine of the world,   10
Ahead of your time, into life.
I will not say—
Go slow.

                    EUGENE McCARTHY

   Even as you read the poem you sense that more is happening than
just an ordinary bicycle ride. Phrases like "pedals of no return," "the
bicycle of your will," and "the spine of the world" make this common
sight represent something much more sweeping—the experience of
growing up.
   Something similar happens in the next poem.

HOUSES

The dentists dig deep to extract
old houses from the city's jaw—
they remove the rotting brick roots,
mess around with the disease-puss of the sewers,
their pneumatic drills explore the aching caverns
before the wounds are allowed to heal—
and then they build a gleaming
white skyline of false teeth
not rooted in the jawbone of tradition
but whole rows juggled   10
on a precarious dental plate.

                    JOHN LACHS

The common and painful experience of a visit to the dentist becomes a way of talking about—or a metaphor for—the human misery, not merely the material facts, of urban renewal. The details of dental work parallel the removal of old rotting houses. The false teeth do not merely replace the old ones but come to stand for the false appearance of a city that is physically, but not morally, "renewed."

Response 17

Coleman Barks characterizes parts of the human body by describing them as other things, often with bizarre humor.

BIG TOE

running running
running   but clean
as a referee's whistle

& absolutely still
within my shoe
inside my sock:

he listens for mud

CAVITIES

the scraps of old
addresses we carry
in our wallets

APPENDIX

one boxing glove
laced up
and ready

GOOSEPIMPLES

crowdpleasers
coming down the aisles
of my arms and legs:

crowds of the pleased
stand up and clap

BRUISES

paint samples
> COLEMAN BARKS

Not only are Barks' comparisons unusual, but so are the parts of the body he chooses to describe. Let these poems suggest ways in which you can describe other parts of the body, as many as you wish. Try to be as imaginative and as fresh as Coleman Barks in both your choices and your descriptions.

Both literal and metaphoric details can be used to make or to imply a definition—especially when the thing defined is not simply a word but a complex idea or feeling. Theodore Roethke defines an emotion by placing before the reader the constant details of offices—the switchboard, multigraph, and paper clip—to suggest the heavy loneliness that comes from their "rituals," their "long afternoons of tedium."

DOLOR

I have known the inexorable sadness of pencils,
Neat in their boxes, dolor of pad and paper-weight,
All the misery of manilla folders and mucilage,
Desolation in immaculate public places,
Lonely reception room, lavatory, switchboard,

The unalterable pathos of basin and pitcher,
Ritual of multigraph, paper-clip, comma,
Endless duplication of lives and objects.
And I have seen dust from the walls of institutions,
Finer than flour, alive, more dangerous than silica,   10
Sift, almost invisible, through long afternoons of tedium,
Dropping a fine film on nails and delicate eyebrows,
Glazing the pale hair, the duplicate gray standard faces.

THEODORE ROETHKE

Don L. Lee presents a sequence of short scenes or "sketches" that provide, by the end of his poem, a definition of black survival. The graphic details in these sketches seem at first to indicate only death and defeat, but they finally imply by contrast the strength of black people who have survived in spite of it all.

MIXED SKETCHES

u feel that way sometimes
wondering:
as a nine year old sister
with burned out hair oddly
smiles at you and sweetly calls you
brother.

u feel that way sometimes
wondering:
as a blackwoman & her 6 children
are burned out of their apartment with no place   10
to go & a nappy-headed nigger comes running thru
our neighborhood with a match in his hand cryin
revolution.

u feel that way sometimes
wondering:
seeing sisters in two hundred dollar wigs & suits
fastmoving in black clubs in late surroundings   talking
about late thoughts in late language waiting for late men
that come in with, "i don't want to hear bout nothing black
    tonight."

u feel that way sometimes   20
wondering:
while eating on newspaper tablecloths
& sleeping on clean bed sheets that couldn't
stop bed bugs   as black children watch their
mothers leave the special buses returning from
special neighborhoods
to clean their "own" unspecial homes.
u feel that way sometimes
wondering:
wondering, how did we survive?   30

                              DON L. LEE

ℛesponse 18

Write a poem in which you try to define an idea as Don L. Lee does black survival or as Theodore Roethke defines dolor. You might have an angle of your own on one of these subjects, or you might try to capture in specific details such abstractions as happiness, the American Dream, fear, poverty, or sex appeal. Name your subject, as Roethke and Lee do, only in the title or in one line. Let your details put your idea across. Because you are working with the various senses, maybe you would like to try presenting your idea in a completely different artistic medium, like dance, painting, or music.

If you've made a list of details before writing your poems, you've probably discovered that the order in which you think of them isn't necessarily the order that presents them best. Here are two short poems, each a sentence long, that order details effectively.

YOUNG WOMAN AT A WINDOW

She sits with
tears on

her cheek
her cheek on

her hand
the child

in her lap
his nose

pressed
to the glass   10

      WILLIAM CARLOS WILLIAMS

DETAILS: SIGHTS, SMELLS, TEXTURES

CHRISTMAS MORNING I

Christmas morning i
got up before the others and
ran
naked across the plank
floor into the front
room to see grandmama
sewing a new
button on my last year
ragdoll.

CAROL FREEMAN

Williams' last word, "glass," sums up the young mother's isolation; even though the window is transparent, it is a hard and effective barrier. Carol Freeman's last word, "ragdoll," emphasizes both her childhood poverty and her grandmother's devotion.

ℜesponse 19

Using "Young Woman at a Window" and "Christmas morning i" as models, write a one-sentence poem that organizes details toward a climax. As these poems show, either something observed or something experienced can be a good subject; the choice is yours.

A strategic arrangement of details is also important in longer poems, where a chaotic pile-up of them could be confusing. The resulting tangle could bury the poet's main point instead of revealing it.

OTHER LIVES

You see them from train windows
in little towns, in those solitary lights
all across Nebraska, in the mysteries
of backyards outside cities—

a single face looking up,
blurred and still as a photograph.
They come to life quickly
in gas stations, overheard in diners,

loom up and dwindle, families
from dreams like memories too
far back to hold. Driving by
you go out to all those strange

10

rooms, all those drawn shades,
those huddled taverns on the highway,
cars nosed-in so close they seem
to touch. And they always snap shut,

fall into the past forever, vast lives
over in an instant. You feed
on this shortness, this mystery
of nearness and regret—such lives

20

so brief you seem immortal;
and you feed, too, on that old hope—
dim as a half-remembered
phone number—that somewhere

people are as you were always
told they were—people who swim
in certainty, who believe, who age
with precision, growing gray like

actors in a high school play.

                    VERN RUTSALA

    The first stanza states the subject: the glimpses of other people's
lives that we get when traveling by train, bus, or car. The sequence of
scenes—backyard, gas station, diner, tavern—slips by as such scenes
do in our experience, giving way to the poet's speculation, which is
brought down to earth by comparing it to a half-remembered phone
number. He wonders if those glimpsed lives have a coherence that his
own lacks, if they make sense in a way life is supposed to but generally

DETAILS: SIGHTS, SMELLS, TEXTURES

doesn't. The final detail, however, calls the "hope" into question: "actors in a high school play" are the representatives of illusion rather than reality, and usually an unconvincing illusion besides. The "people who swim / in certainty" are a dream: "people . . . as you were always told they were" exist only in our imaginations.

Such a reversal can be comic as well as serious. The next poem amusingly exposes a housewife's experience of a repeated frustration. She "carries on" at first as if she were making a sharp break from her ordinary life, but we find in the last line that her rebellion is really a part of her routine after all.

SOMETIMES MY HUSBAND

Sometimes my husband
acts
just like a man . . .

dishes are evil / you know
they can destroy the spirit . . .

Washing dishes should
be outlawed

paper plate nirvana!

long live dixie cups!

     . . . tomorrow i am going to lose   10
       my temper—

       i will destroy all the dishes
       that i missed last week—

          PATRICIA PARKER

Here is another poem that relies on a sudden switch for its punch.

ONE THOUSAND NINE HUNDRED & SIXTY-EIGHT WINTERS

Got up this morning
Feeling good & black
Thinking black thoughts
Did black things
Played all my black records
And minded my own black business
Put on my best black clothes
Walked out my black door
And, Lord have mercy: white snow!

JACI EARLEY

ℛesponse 20

Choose one of the poems that you have written for the Responses in this chapter and, looking at it from another angle, rewrite it so that a reversal of thought or feeling hits your reader in the final lines.

Poems
to read and discuss

THE MAN IN THE DEAD MACHINE

High on a slope in New Guinea
the Grumann Hellcat
lodges among bright vines
as thick as arms. In 1943
the clenched hand of a pilot
glided it here
where no one has ever been.

In the cockpit the helmeted
skeleton sits
upright, held   10
by dry sinews at neck
and shoulder, and webbing
that straps the pelvic cross
to the cracked
leather of the seat, and the breastbone
to the canvas cover
of the parachute.

Or say that the shrapnel
missed him, he flew
back to the carrier, and every   20
morning takes the train, his pale
hands on his black case, and sits
upright, held
by the firm webbing.

                DONALD HALL

NUMBER 5—DECEMBER

Nobody knows me
when I go round
late at night
scratching on windows
& whispering in hallways
looking for someone
who loves me in the daytime
to take me in
at night

DAVID HENDERSON

THE CRIPPLING

I used to watch
it on the ledge:
a crippled bird.
Surely it would
die soon.
Then I saw a man
at one of the windows
fed it a few seeds,
a crust from lunch.
Often he forgot   10
and it went hopping on the ledge
a starving scurvy sparrow.
Every couple of weeks
he caught it in his hand
and clipped back one wing.
I call it a sparrow.
The plumage was sooty.
Sometimes in the sun
the feathers might have
been scarlet like a tanager.   20
He never
let it fly.
He never took it in.
Perhaps he was starving himself.

Perhaps he counted
every crumb.
Perhaps he hated
that anything live
knew how to fly.

MARGE PIERCY

HARRY WILMANS

I was just turned twenty-one,
And Henry Phipps, the Sunday-school superintendent,
Made a speech in Bindle's Opera House.
"The honor of the flag must be upheld," he said,
"Whether it be assailed by a barbarous tribe of Tagalogs
Or the greatest power in Europe."
And we cheered and cheered the speech and the flag he
    waved
As he spoke.
And I went to the war in spite of my father,
And followed the flag till I saw it raised   10
By our camp in a rice field near Manila,
And all of us cheered and cheered it.
But there were flies and poisonous things;
And there was the deadly water,
And the cruel heat,
And the sickening, putrid food;
And the smell of the trench just back of the tents
Where the soldiers went to empty themselves;
And there were the whores who followed us, full of syphilis;
And beastly acts between ourselves or alone,   20
With bullying, hatred, degradation among us,
And days of loathing and nights of fear
To the hour of the charge through the steaming swamp,
Following the flag,
Till I fell with a scream, shot through the guts.
Now there's a flag over me in Spoon River!
A flag! A flag!

EDGAR LEE MASTERS

POEM IN WHICH MY LEGS ARE ACCEPTED

Legs!
How we have suffered each other,
never meeting the standards of magazines
or official measurements.

I have hung you from trapezes,
sat you on wooden rollers,
pulled and pushed you
with the anxiety of taffy,
and still, you are yourselves!

Most obvious imperfection, blight on my fantasy life,   10
strong,
plump,
never to be skinny
or even hinting of the svelte beauties in history books
or Sears catalogues.
Here you are—solid, fleshy and
white as when I first noticed you, sitting on the toilet,
spread softly over the
wooden seat,
having been with me only twelve years,   20

                                    yet
as obvious as the legs of my thirty-year-old gym teacher.

Legs!
O that was the year we did acrobatics in the annual gym show.
How you split for me!
                    One-handed cartwheels
                    from this end of the gymnasium to the
                        other,
                    ending in double splits,
legs you flashed in blue rayon slacks my mother bought for
    the occasion
and tho you were confidently swinging along,   30
the rest of me blushed at the sound of clapping.

Legs!
How I have worried about you, not able to hide you,
embarrassed at beaches, in highschool
                    when the cheerleaders' slim brown legs
                                spread all over
                                the sand
                                with the perfection
                                of bamboo.
I hated you, and still you have never given out on me.   40

With you
I have risen to the top of blue waves,
with you
I have carried food home as a loving gift
                            when my arms began un-
                            jelling like madrilenne.

Legs, you are a pillow,
white and plentiful with feathers for his wild head.
You are the endless scenery
behind the tense sinewy elegance of his two dark legs.   50
You welcome him joyfully
and dance.
And you will be the locks in a new canal between continents.
            The ship of life will push out of you
            and rejoice
                in the whiteness,
                in the first floating and rising of water.

                                    KATHLEEN FRASER

A WOMAN'S COMPLAINT

What shall I do? My man compares me
to a wild red flower.
When I have withered in his hands,
he will leave me.

AMERICAN INDIAN, AZTEC, TRADITIONAL

A BEAUTIFUL YOUNG NYMPH GOING TO BED

Corinna, Pride of *Drury-Lane,*
For whom no Shepherd sighs in vain;
Never did *Covent Garden* boast
So bright a batter'd, strolling Toast;
No drunken Rake to pick her up,
No Cellar where on Tick to sup;
Returning at the Midnight Hour;
Four Stories climbing to her Bow'r;
Then, seated on a three-legg'd Chair,
Takes off her artificial Hair: 10
Now, picking out a Crystal Eye,
She wipes it clean, and lays it by.
Her Eye-Brows from a Mouse's Hyde,
Stuck on with Art on either Side,
Pulls off with Care, and first displays 'em,
Then in a Play-Book smoothly lays 'em.
Now dextrously her Plumpers draws,
That serve to fill her hollow Jaws.
Untwists a Wire; and from her Gums
A Set of Teeth completely comes.   20
Pulls out the Rags contriv'd to prop
Her flabby Dugs and down they drop.
Proceeding on, the lovely Goddess
Unlaces next her Steel-Rib'd Bodice;
Which by the Operator's Skill,
Press down the Lumps, the Hollows fill,
Up goes her Hand, and off she slips
The Bolsters that supply her Hips.
With gentlest Touch, she next explores
Her Shankers, Issues, running Sores,   30
Effects of many a sad Disaster;
And then to each applies a Plaister.

But must, before she goes to Bed,
Rub off the Dawbs of White and Red;
And smooth the Furrows in her Front,
With greasy Paper stuck upon't.
She takes a *Bolus* e'er she sleeps;
And then between two Blankets creeps.
With Pains of Love tormented lies;
Or if she chance to close her Eyes,   40
Of *Bridewell* and the *Compter* dreams,
And feels the Lash, and faintly screams;
Or, by a faithless Bully drawn,
At some Hedge-Tavern lies in Pawn;
Or to *Jamaica* seems transported,
Alone, and by no Planter courted;
Or, near *Fleet-Ditch's* oozy Brinks,
Surrounded with a Hundred Stinks,
Belated, seems on watch to lye,
And snap some Cully passing by;   50
Or, struck with Fear, her Fancy runs
On Watchmen, Constables and Duns,
From whom she meets with frequent Rubs;
But, never from Religious Clubs;
Whose Favour she is sure to find,
Because she pays them all in Kind.
    Corinna wakes. A dreadful Sight!
Behold the Ruins of the Night!
A wicked Rat her Plaister stole,
Half eat, and dragg'd it to his Hole.   60
The Crystal Eye, alas, was miss't;
And *Puss* had on her Plumpers pisst.
A Pigeon pick'd her Issue-Peas;
And *Shock* her Tresses fill'd with Fleas.
    The Nymph, tho' in this mangled Plight,
Must ev'ry Morn her Limbs unite.
But how shall I describe her Arts
To recollect the scatter'd Parts?
Or shew the Anguish, Toil, and Pain,
Of gath'ring up herself again?   70
The bashful Muse will never bear
In such a Scene to interfere.
Corinna in the Morning dizen'd,
Who sees, will spew; who smells, be poison'd.

JONATHAN SWIFT

THE DOLL BELIEVERS

This lifeless construction,
Yellow hair curled and twisted,
The forever motionless face of rubber,
The dark marked eyebrows,
The pug nose of flexible material,
Spongy cheeks painted red,
Camel-hair eyebrows moving up and down.
Lifting her up, the eyes fly open,
They stare into space unmoved,
Those deep blue and soft eyes,   10
Those never winking, moving balls,
Controlled from the inside,
And that thick rubber body,
The imprint of a navel,
The undersized hands,
The thick soft knees,
The screwed-on head,
The air hole behind her neck,
All this in its lifelessness
Gives me a feeling that children   20
Are really powerful people
To imagine that such a thing
Could be alive.

                          CLARENCE MAJOR

GAME AFTER SUPPER

This is before electricity,
it is when there were porches.

On the sagging porch an old man
is rocking. The porch is wooden,

the house is wooden and grey;
in the living room which smells of
smoke and mildew, soon
the woman will light the kerosene lamp.

There is a barn but I am not in the barn;
there is an orchard too, gone bad,   10

its apples like soft cork
but I am not there either.

I am hiding in the long grass
with my two dead cousins,
the membrane grown already
across their throats.

We hear crickets and our own hearts
close to our ears;
though we giggle, we are afraid.

From the shadows around   20
the corner of the house
a tall man is coming to find us:

He will be an uncle,
if we are lucky.

MARGARET ATWOOD

EPISTLE

To Miss Blount
On Her Leaving the Town After the Coronation

As some fond virgin, whom her mother's care
Drags from the town to wholesome country air,
Just when she learns to roll a melting eye,
And hear a spark, yet think no danger nigh;
From the dear man unwilling she must sever,
Yet takes one kiss before she parts for ever:
Thus from the world fair Zephalinda flew,
Saw others happy, and with sighs withdrew;
Not that their pleasures caus'd her discontent,
She sigh'd not that They stay'd, but that She went.   10
   She went, to plain-work, and to purling brooks,
Old-fashion'd halls, dull aunts, and croaking rooks:
She went from Op'ra, park, assembly, play,
To morning-walks, and pray'rs three hours a day;
To part her time 'twixt reading and Bohea,
To muse, and spill her solitary Tea,
Or o'er cold coffee trifle with the spoon,

Count the slow clock, and dine exact at noon;
Divert her eyes with pictures in the fire,
Hum half a tune, tell stories to the squire;   20
Up to her godly garret after sev'n,
There starve and pray, for that's the way to heav'n.
   Some Squire, perhaps, you take delight to rack;
Whose game is Whisk, whose treat a toast in sack;
Who visits with a gun, presents you birds,
Then gives a smacking buss, and cries,—No words!
Or with his hound comes hallowing from the stable,
Makes love with nods, and knees beneath a table;
Whose laughs are hearty, tho' his jests are coarse,
And loves you best of all things—but his horse.   30
   In some fair ev'ning, on your elbow laid,
You dream of triumphs in the rural shade;
In pensive thought recall the fancy'd scene,
See Coronations rise on ev'ry green;
Before you pass th' imaginary sights
Of Lords, and Earls, and Dukes, and garter'd Knights,
While the spread Fan o'ershades your closing eyes;
Then give one flirt, and all the vision flies.
Thus vanish sceptres, coronets, and balls,
And leave you in lone woods, or empty walls!   40
   So when your slave, at some dear idle time,
(Not plagu'd with head-achs, or the want of rhyme)
Stands in the streets, abstracted from the crew,
And while he seems to study, thinks of you;
Just when his fancy points your sprightly eyes,
Or sees the blush of soft Parthenia rise,
Gay pats my shoulder, and you vanish quite,
Streets, chairs, and coxcombs rush upon my sight;
Vex'd to be still in town, I knit my brow,
Look sour, and hum a tune, as you may now.   50

                              ALEXANDER POPE

STRAY ANIMALS

This is the beauty of being alone
toward the end of summer:
a dozen stray animals asleep on the porch
in the shade of my feet,

and the smell of leaves burning
in another neighborhood.
It is late morning,
and my forehead is alive with shadows,
some bats rock back and forth
to the rhythm of my humming,   10
the mimosa flutters with bees.
This is a house of unwritten poems,
this is where I am unborn.

                              JAMES TATE

MORNING HALF-LIFE BLUES

Girls buck the wind in the grooves toward work
in fuzzy coats promised to be warm as fur.
The shop windows snicker
flashing them hurrying over dresses they cannot afford:
you are not pretty enough, not pretty enough.

Blown with yesterday's papers through the boiled coffee
    morning
they dream of the stop on the subway without a name,
the door in the heart of the grove of skyscrapers,
that garden where we nestle to the teats of a furry world,
lie in mounds of peony eating grapes,   10
and need barter ourselves for nothing,
not by the hour, not by the pound, not by the skinful,
that party to which no one will give or sell them the key
though we have all thought briefly we had found it
drunk or in bed.

Black girls with thin legs and high necks stalking like herons,
plump girls with blue legs and green eyelids and strawberry
    breasts,
swept off to be frozen in fluorescent cubes,
the vacuum of your jobs sucks your brains dry
and fills you with the ooze of melted comics.   20
Living is later. This is your rented death.
You grasp at specific commodities and vague lusts
to make up, to pay for each day
which opens like a can and is empty, and then another,
afternoons like dinosaur eggs stuffed with glue.

Girls of the dirty morning, ticketed and spent,
you will be less at forty than at twenty.
Your living is a waste product of somebody's mill.
I would fix you like buds to a city where people work
to make and do things necessary and good,   30
where work is real as bread and babies and trees in parks
and you would blossom slowly and ripen to sound fruit.

                                        MARGE PIERCY

THE HUNCHBACK IN THE PARK

The hunchback in the park
A solitary mister
Propped between trees and water
From the opening of the garden lock
That lets the trees and water enter
Until the Sunday sombre bell at dark

Eating bread from a newspaper
Drinking water from the chained cup
That the children filled with gravel
In the fountain basin where I sailed my ship   10
Slept at night in a dog kennel
But nobody chained him up.

Like the park birds he came early
Like the water he sat down
And Mister they called Hey mister
The truant boys from the town
Running when he had heard them clearly
On out of sound

Past lake and rockery
Laughing when he shook his paper   20
Hunchbacked in mockery
Through the loud zoo of the willow groves
Dodging the park keeper
With his stick that picked up leaves.

And the old dog sleeper
Alone between nurses and swans
While the boys among willows

Made the tigers jump out of their eyes
To roar on the rockery stones
And the groves were blue with sailors   30

Made all day until bell time
A woman figure without fault
Straight as a young elm
Straight and tall from his crooked bones
That she might stand in the night
After the locks and chains

All night in the unmade park
After the railings and shrubberies
The birds the grass the trees the lake
And the wild boys innocent as strawberries   40
Had followed the hunchback
To his kennel in the dark.

                              DYLAN THOMAS

SAMANTHA IS MY NEGRO CAT

Samantha is my
Negro cat.
Black with yellow eyes.
A big flat nose.
Thick features.
She came to me
from the street.
(A street nigger
with hairless ears.)
She's tough.   10
Been a mother too.
Has hard pink nipples.
(Yes, pink. She also has
a white spot on her neck.
She ain't pure. But
I don't care. I ain't no racist.)
She has a sad high ass.
Sway-back.
Not much to look at

but as affectionate   20
as any girl who's
had a hard time of it.
"Bums," said the vet
a little too objectively,
"always respond to love."

Samantha rubs against
me, sits across my
lap, purring her short-circuited purr.

Lady, this man is
going to treat you better   30
than the rest.
(You say you've heard that one before.)
We'll comfort each other
in the evenings
after supper, when we stare
out on the
cold and dark street.

                        WILLIAM J. HARRIS

WHEN IT WAS COLD

When it was cold
before the war
and the wind would
whistle
through our house
like it was in a hurry
to get through
but it had to leave its
message
I used to wonder   10
why we was the only
ones
getting messages
from the wind.

        FRANK LAMONT PHILLIPS

HIGHWAY 5 TOWARD VANCOUVER

July and the windows open,
through country indifferent as film
the wheels sway, a leaf hasn't time to tick
nor ripple widen; dust of a distant
bulldozer like whipped cream
freezes on the horizon.

You blink away the human obstinacy
of feet lifting,
one after another,
love and despair in tempo.   10
That foot will not fall
across the fence of the impervious concrete

nor pebble click
through its sound barrier.
Only the passing roar
of familiar engines
blurs your preoccupation
in the raw components of travel.

Imagine your life like that,
the swift road north,   20
bypassing the major and terrible cities,
no back streets to curve you over and over
some intricate disaster.
You are occasionally muddled perhaps
by an indifferent signpost or lose
a few minutes to road under construction.

At night risking animal shadows,
catacylsmic skids on the skin
of wet pavement, you are calmed
by the intimate dimming of headlights.   30

To be going, going, somewhere,
sure of the ultimate truth of your destination,
or if not sure exactly at least committed
to one hurtling direction:

116

America, north star, I am young,
younger than thirty.
In your way I stand, passionate,
baffled, step caught in crossing.
There is a swath of grey in my hair
that curves like that promising freeway.   40

FRANCES McCONNEL

SONNET 130

My mistress' eyes are nothing like the sun;
Coral is far more red than her lips' red;
If snow be white, why then her breasts are dun;
If hairs be wires, black wires grow on her head.
I have seen roses damasked, red and white,
But no such roses see I in her cheeks,
And in some perfumes is there more delight
Than in the breath that from my mistress reeks.
I love to hear her speak, yet well I know
That music hath a far more pleasing sound.   10
I grant I never saw a goddess go;
My mistress when she walks treads on the ground.
    And yet, by heaven, I think my love as rare
    As any she belied with false compare.

WILLIAM SHAKESPEARE

DISABLED

He sat in a wheeled chair, waiting for dark,
And shivered in his ghastly suit of grey,
Legless, sewn short at elbow. Through the park
Voices of boys rang saddening like a hymn,
Voices of play and pleasures after day,
Till gathering sleep had mothered them from him.

About this time Town used to swing so gay
When glow-lamps budded in the light blue trees,
And girls glanced lovelier as the air grew dim,—

In the old times, before he threw away his knees.   10
Now he will never feel again how slim
Girls' waists are, or how warm their subtle hands;
All of them touch him like some queer disease.

There was an artist silly for his face,
For it was younger than his youth, last year.
Now, he is old; his back will never brace;
He's lost his colour very far from here,
Poured it down shell-holes till the veins ran dry,
And half his lifetime lapsed in the hot race,
And leap of purple spurted from his thigh.   20

One time he liked a blood-smear down his leg,
After the matches, carried shoulder-high.
It was after football, when he'd drunk a peg,
He thought he'd better join.—He wonders why.
Someone had said he'd look a god in kilts,
That's why; and may be, too, to please his Meg;
Aye, that was it, to please the giddy jilts
He asked to join. He didn't have to beg;
Smiling they wrote his lie; aged nineteen years.
Germans he scarcely thought of; all their guilt,   30
And Austria's, did not move him. And no fears
Of Fear came yet. He thought of jewelled hilts
For daggers in plain socks; of smart salutes;
And care of arms; and leave; and pay arrears;
Esprit de corps; and hints for young recruits.
And soon he was drafted out with drums and cheers.

Some cheered him home, but not as crowds cheer Goal.
Only a solemn man who brought him fruits
Thanked him; and then inquired about his soul.

Now, he will spend a few sick years in Institutes,   40
And do what things the rules consider wise,
And take whatever pity they may dole.
To-night he noticed how the women's eyes
Passed from him to the strong men that were whole.
How cold and late it is! Why don't they come
And put him into bed? Why don't they come?

WILFRED OWEN

OPTIONS

Rank on rank of false right eyes
Stared into my loss
And I saw
He would not find my soft brown eye,
Not in a thousand leather trays;
Not for all the purple velvet
That could be cut to lay them on
Was there an option
Able to resplit my sight
Or make me a king.   10
Not even his costly Orientals
Could fake my lost right eye.

He tried, eye after eye;
They lay like bogus coins
In my forehead.

Level with his window was a minaret
On whose globe he said
To fix my fluid left eye
For a truer fit.
As he ground with sand and steel   20
To shape blown glass to my blind side,
I saw again the world no longer turned
Around the sun,
Was flat, lacked depth,
Went neither beyond
Nor came before
The one-dimensional plane
Of sky and globe and minaret.

Into that vacancy
He placed the cold brown eye   30
My father paid him money for.
It was like a slug in the musicbox;
I could not play my song.
When I reached for things
They still were not there.

In the mirror beside his window
I tried again to find a true brown eye;
The truest there
Was in my father's saddened face.
Through the dark prosthetic glass   40
Vision came of my sovereign option:
I broke from his hand,
The stranger's vitreous smile, that humorless room,
And went into the park below.
Bell notes floated from the minaret
Like concentric waves in the fountain pool
Where I threw the mold-blown piece
And began to sort the planes,
Play the songs,
Between sky and globe and minaret,   50
Trusting depth to the patch of black
Behind my lost brown eye.

JAMES SEAY

5
Shapes

Sounds, rhythms, details—all touch our senses at every moment of our lives; even our sleep is affected by dream images and the rhythms of breath and heartbeat. A poet, in order to separate his poem from all the data he draws on and thus make a distinct impression on his readers, must somehow organize his poetic material, give it form, give it its own unique shape.

Most obviously, he arranges words into lines of varying length, and by doing so emphasizes elements of special significance. In the following poem, the desperate mechanical repetitiveness of the miner's life makes its impact through the poet's arrangement of the lines. The abrupt, ironically contrasting lines, "a black corpse" and "a white corpse," present a static image of death that makes the miner's activity —returning from the mine, washing, eating dinner—seem futile. Although the miner is partially restored to life by his meal, no longer merely a "white corpse," his restoration is not complete. The abrupt last line sums up his new life in the negative phrase "not hungry."

HE RETURNED FROM THE MINE

he returned from the mine
   a black corpse.
he washed and came
   to the table
a white corpse.

```
    sunken eyes glowing
intensely ribs
    heaving cheeks hollow
and pale.
    he ate roast beef corn                              10
peas salad baked
    potato; drank milk.
Smiling eyes steady
    breathing not so
pale and hollow.
    Not anymore thank you
not hungry.
```

MARGARET ECKMAN

ℛesponse 21

PARENTS

Linda failed to return home from a dance Friday night.
On Saturday
she admitted she had spent the night
with an Air Force lieutenant.

The Aults decided on a punishment
that would "wake Linda up."
They ordered her
to shoot the dog
she had owned about two years.
On Sunday,   10
the Aults and
Linda
took the dog into the desert
near their home.
They
had the girl
dig a shallow grave.
Then
Mrs. Ault
grasped the dog between her hands and   20

Mr. Ault
gave
his daughter
a .22 caliber pistol
and told her
to shoot the dog.

Instead,
the girl
put the pistol
to her right temple   30
and shot herself.

The police said
there were no charges
that could be filed
against the parents
except possibly

cruelty
to
animals.

(*The New York Times*—February 7, 1968)

JULIUS LESTER

THE WAR—II

Mrs. John Smith of Nashville, Tenn.,
the wife of a cameraman
for the Columbia Broadcasting System,
has been living in the Caravelle
for nearly a year.

From her terrace
she watched
tanks and troops
move beneath her,
watched the barbed wire   10
drawn into a net
around the National Assembly Building

across the street,
watched
two truckloads
of dead Americans
being driven by.

"It was the
first time
I've ever seen   20
so many
dead people
at once,"

she said.

(*The New York Times*—February 3, 1968)

                    JULIUS LESTER

These "poems" were originally newspaper reports. Julius Lester has turned them into a new kind of poetry called "found poetry." He explains: "We are so accustomed to reading horror in each day's newspapers, the news columns bordered by ads, that we have become insensitive to that horror. By taking news articles and arranging them as poems, what was mere news in one context becomes the human experience it really is."

First try to explain to yourself why Julius Lester arranges the lines in each story as he does; why he wants you to read on without a break in some places and to pause in others. Why, for example, does he divide the phrase "cruelty to animals" into three lines at the end of "Parents"?

Then, using any current newspaper or news magazine, find an item that seems to you to have human interest, and arrange it into lines that will bring out the impact you feel the statement in the news item really should have.

Sometimes the poet arranges his lines so that their shape almost gives a picture of its subject matter. William Carlos Williams' "Poem" helps you to read about and also to visualize, either in imagination or in memory, the delicate precision of a cat making its way through a cluttered space. Each new line is a calculated stage in the cat's progress; the animal moves as slowly and deliberately as the short lines do.

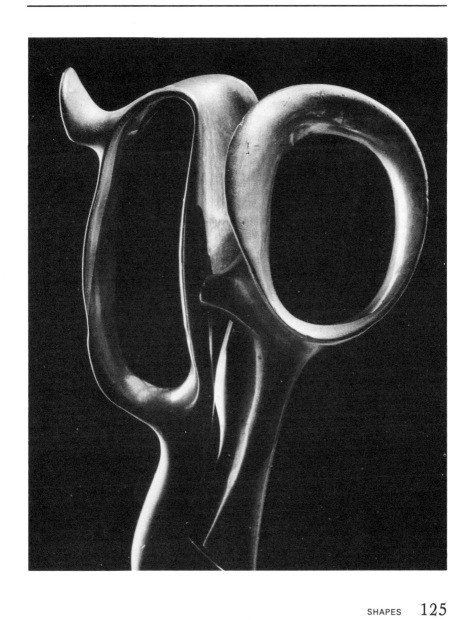

POEM

As the cat
climbed over
the top of

the jamcloset
first the right
forefoot

carefully
then the hind
stepped down

into the pit of   10
the empty
flowerpot

    WILLIAM CARLOS WILLIAMS

As you've probably noticed, the lines of a poem don't all have to be-
gin at the left-hand margin. They can be laid out all over the page, as in
the next poem.

MERRITT PARKWAY

    As if it were
forever that they move, that we
    keep moving—

        Under a wan sky where
        as the lights went on a star
            pierced the haze and now
        follows steadily
                a constant
        above our six lanes
        the dreamlike continuum . . .   10

And the people—ourselves!
    the humans from inside the
    cars, apparent
    only at gasoline stops
                unsure,
        eyeing each other

                    drink coffee hastily at the
                    slot machines and hurry
                  back to the cars
                        vanish   20
                        into them forever, to
                        keep moving—

Houses now and then beyond the
sealed road, the trees/trees, bushes
passing by, passing
            the cars that
            keep moving ahead of

        us, past us, pressing behind us
                                    and
                    over left, those that come   30
                toward us shining too brightly
moving relentlessly

            in six lanes, gliding
            north and south, speeding with
            a slurred sound—

                    DENISE LEVERTOV

If you think of traffic on a highway as moving steadily forward, the
arrangement of lines in this poem will at first seem pointless. Denise
Levertov's subject, however, is not traffic as seen from above or out-
side. It is, instead, traffic as experienced by a traveler on the highway.
The irregular pattern of the lines follows her different sequences of
thought. The lines beginning

                Under a wan sky where
                as the lights went on a star
                        pierced the haze and now
                follows steadily

are set further in and apart from the opening of the poem to represent
the "dreamlike" state of mind of the bored and isolated travelers. The
word "pierced" is set still further in because it corresponds to a small
break in the monotony—a star pierces the haze. Look at the whole
poem again. The reader's eyes must hurry after the hasty movements
of the travelers' rest stop. Also, notice the word "unsure," standing

by itself in the middle of the poem, and the sudden regularity of the margin after the travelers have rushed back to the cars. Can you account for their placement in the poem and for any other irregularities that strike you?

Sometimes a line arrangement literally pictures a poem's subject. This extreme use of shape is usually frivolous, but in the following poem, by a seventeenth-century poet, the technique is used seriously.

EASTER WINGS

Lord, who createdst man in wealth and store,
    Though foolishly he lost the same,
        Decaying more and more
            Till he became
             Most poor:
             With thee
           O let me rise
        As larks, harmoniously,
    And sing this day thy victories:
Then shall the fall further the flight in me.   10

My tender age in sorrow did begin:
    And still with sicknesses and shame
        Thou didst so punish sin,
            That I became
             Most thin.
             With thee
           Let me combine,
        And feel this day thy victory:
    For, if I imp my wing on thine,
Affliction shall advance the flight in me.   20

                    GEORGE HERBERT

When the speaker feels himself "most poor" and "most thin," the line, like his spirit, contracts as much as possible. The lines grow smaller as sin makes inroads on the speaker's happiness and wholeness; they expand as divine grace lifts him to his share in God's victory. His soul rises like a bird in flight, and "wings" become the symbol of his salvation.

Some poets still try seriously to fuse poetry—"words"—with physical shapes in an effort to support their meaning, as in the following poem. Begin reading at the center of the diagram.

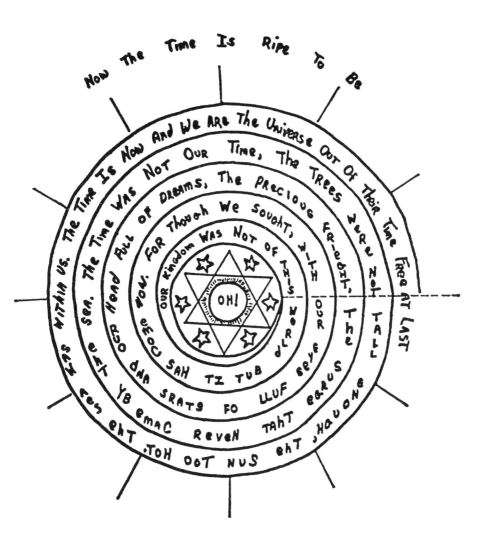

JOE GONCALVES

ℜesponse 22

Write a poem, as serious or as playful as you choose, that makes use of, or sketches, a physical shape. Either a very obvious subject, like a bird or a house, is possible, or a very abstract one, perhaps something that expresses physically a common phrase like "going around in circles" or "going to pieces."

The shape the poet gives his poem can help him organize his ideas and experiences in a way that will communicate them to his readers. Nikki Giovanni's "Alabama Poem" illustrates such a use of shape. To introduce each new experience she reverses the usual paragraph indentation. The extended line also acts as a clue to the reader to follow the poet's eye toward what has attracted it: the trees, the old man, the old woman, and the trees again.

ALABAMA POEM

if trees could talk
   wonder what they'd say
met an old man
   on the road late after noon
   hat pulled over to shade
   his eyes
   jacket slumped over his
   shoulders
   told me "girl! my hands seen
   more than all   10
   them books they got
   at tuskegee"
   smiled at me
   half waved his hand
   walked on down the dusty road
met an old woman
   with a corncob pipe
   sitting and rocking
   on a spring evening

"sista" she called to me   20
"let me tell you—my feet
seen more than yo eyes
ever gonna read"
smiled at her and kept
on moving
gave it a thought and went
back to the porch
"i say gal" she called down
"you a student at the institute?
better come here and study   30
these feet
i'm gonna cut a bunion off
soons i gets up"
i looked at her
she laughed at me
if trees would talk
wonder what they'd tell me

                                    NIKKI GIOVANNI

Line groupings can help to communicate sequences of events and sensations. Chad Walsh emphasizes the bitterness with which he sees the suburban executives' daily round by breaking it down into a succession of two-line pictures. Each moment is frozen like a snapshot.

PORT AUTHORITY TERMINAL: 9 A.M. MONDAY

From buses beached like an invasion fleet
They fill the waiting room with striding feet.

Their faces, white, and void of hate or pity,
Move on tall bodies toward the conquered city.

Among the lesser breeds of black and brown
They board their taxis with an absent frown,

Each to his concrete citadel,
To rule the city and to buy and sell.

At five o'clock they ride the buses back,
Leaving their Irish to guard the brown and black.   10

At six a drink, at seven dinner's served.
At ten or twelve, depressed, undressed, unnerved,

They mount their wives, dismount, they doze and dream
Apocalyptic Negroes in a stream

Of moving torches, marching from the slums,
Beating a band of garbage pails for drums,

Marching, with school-age children in their arms,
Advancing on the suburbs and the farms,

To integrate the schools and burn the houses . . .
The normal morning comes, the clock arouses   20

Junior and senior executive alike.
Back on the bus, and down the usual pike.

From buses beached like an invasion fleet
They fill the waiting room with striding feet.

                                              CHAD WALSH

Therl Ryan uses groups of three lines. The last two lines in each stanza rhyme to clinch the statement, constructing a series of separate experiences all finally underlining one point, the speaker's hopeless loneliness.

AUTUMN WOMAN

Gusts cry at my window
Hurling in from the sea,
As I watch wearily.

Leaves run red as the sun
Plucked from a summer tree
By autumn thievery.

A miner's homeward bound,
Bent with dusty ills,
From deep wounds in the hills,

Fishermen bind the boat   10
Safe from the heaving shore
And the sea's hungry floor;

A shepherd drives his flock
Beachward and past the foam
Where the sun wanders home.

Hearth is warm and quilts are soft;
The men have left the lea,
But no one comes to me.

                    THERL RYAN

Don L. Lee shapes the poem "Big Momma" in order to guide the reader in a variety of ways. The lines making up the left margin describe the sequence of events, while the indented lines report Big Momma's direct speech. Certain words are stressed by the spacing around them: like "pensionless" and "real teeth" in the first and last lines of the poem. This ordering of elements makes what might seem a formless poem wonderfully clear. There is no need for such direct and dull explanation as "I went for a visit, as I usually do every week, etc." and no need for standard punctuation and capitalization—both of which could dilute what Lee has to say.

BIG MOMMA

finally retired   pensionless
from cleaning somebody else's house
she remained home to clean .
the one she didn't own.

in her kitchen where we often talked
the *chicago tribune* served as a tablecloth
for the two cups of tomato soup that went
along with my weekly visit & talkingto.

she was in a seriously-funny mood
& from the get-go she was down, realdown: 10

     roaches around here are like
     letters on a newspaper
     or
     u gonta be a writer, hunh
     when u gone write me some writen
     or
     the way niggers act around here
     if talk cd kill we'd all be dead.

she's somewhat confused about all this *blackness*
but said that it's good when negroes start putting themselves   20
first and added: we've always shopped at the colored stores,
        & the way niggers cut each other up round
        here every weekend that whiteman don't
           haveta
        worry bout no revolution specially when he's
        gonta haveta pay for it too, anyhow all he's
        gotta do is drop a truck load of *dope* out
           there
        on 43rd st. & all the niggers & yr
           revolutionaries
        be too busy getten high & then they'll turn
           round
        and fight each other over who got the
           mostest.

we finished our soup and i moved to excuse myself,   30
as we walked to the front door she made a last comment:
      now *luther* i knows you done changed a lots but if
      you can think back, we never did eat too much pork
      round here anyways, it was bad for the belly.
i shared her smile and agreed.

touching the snow lightly i headed for 43rd st.
at the corner i saw a brother crying   while
trying to hold up a lamp post,
thru his watery eyes i cd see big momma's words.

at sixty-eight
she moves freely, is often right   40
and when there is food
eats   joyously with her own
real teeth.

                     DON L. LEE

ℛesponse 23

If you try to tell someone about an experience, you often find yourself
bogged down in irrelevant detail: was it Wednesday or Thursday, or
does it matter? Friends are usually patient, however, and allow you to
flounder on to the end, even if you forget the point you set out to make.
Readers of poetry, though, are not. Poets not only need to select de-
tails but also to arrange them in a manner that gives their poems the
sense and force that will hold their readers' attention.

    You have already seen several examples of such ordering; now try
to create one of your own. You may have seen something common-
place that, for you, is somewhat like Walsh's "Port Authority Termi-
nal: 9 a.m. Monday"; if so, try presenting it to your reader in two-
line stanzas like Walsh's, though not necessarily in rhyme. If this
style doesn't appeal to you, try Don L. Lee's instead; describe a
meeting with another person in which the layout of the poem tells
the reader what has happened and who is speaking.

Many poems, of course, have been written in fixed forms, conforming to rules that require a certain number and length of lines, a certain arrangement of rhymes, or all of these at once. Such "rules," naturally, are made up by poets themselves, not by external authorities, and poets are always free to change and modify them. A framework of flexible requirements, however, can help a poet to refine his expression, to concentrate his meaning in a way he might not if he gave himself no restrictions.

Some of these fixed forms are now seldom used, particularly if their rules are so elaborate that they make writing a poem simply a clever trick, like constructing a crossword puzzle. Others, however, have proven both so flexible and so useful in helping to shape the poet's meaning that they continue to be used even as other fashions come and go. Two particularly popular forms that seem to have proven their value are the ballad and the sonnet.

The ballad was originally a musical form, and many of today's song lyrics still use it. Unlike most song lyrics, however, a ballad can usually stand separately from its music and work as a poem. Many traditional ballads have been sung to more than one tune, and composers and musicians sometimes still create new musical settings for them. Clearly a sung ballad with a highly repetitive refrain, particularly a nonsense one ("Down a down, derry, derry, derry, down, down," for example), will look silly printed on a page and probably quickly irritate the reader, but such refrains are usually detachable from the ballad's substance. Other repetitive phrases, however, can still be effective in print, as in the following traditional ballad.

BONNIE GEORGE CAMPBELL

High upon Highlands,
  And low upon Tay,
Bonnie George Campbell
  Rode out on a day;
Saddled and bridled,
  And gallant to see:
Home came his good horse,
  But home came not he.

Out ran his old mother,
  Wild with despair;   10
Out ran his bonnie bride,
  Tearing her hair.

He rode saddled and bridled,
  With boots to the knee:
Home came his good horse,
  But never came he.

"My meadow lies green,
  And my corn is unshorn,
My barn is unbuilt,
  And my babe is unborn."   20
He rode saddled and bridled,
  Careless and free:
Safe home came the saddle,
  But never came he.

ANONYMOUS

While the phrase "saddled and bridled" remains fixed, the refrain is
varied enough—"Home came not he" is replaced by the more definite
"But never came he," both to prevent the reader from becoming bored
and to underscore the finality of Bonnie George Campbell's disappear-
ance. This repetition is directly related to another characteristic of the
ballad form: while the fact of Campbell's disappearance is repeated
again and again, his fate is left unexplained. Ballads tend to focus on,
to light up, a few details that suggest a situation powerfully to the
reader's imagination. What happened to Campbell anyhow? The
obscurity of his fate adds to its emotional effect on the audience.

"Bonnie George Campbell," like most of the older ballads, has no
known author. Presumably it passed orally from one singer to another,
sometimes changing in the process as people forgot some details and
added others. Some poets still use the ballad form, whether or not they
use the four-line stanza. Langston Hughes varies the traditional form
by repeating street names and the opening phrase "Could be."

COULD BE

Could be Hastings Street,
Or Lenox Avenue,
Could be 18th & Vine
And still be true.

Could be 5th & Mound,
Could be Rampart:
When you pawned my watch
You pawned my heart.

Could be you love me,
Could be that you don't.   10
Might be that you'll come back,
Like as not you won't.

Hastings Street is weary,
Also Lenox Avenue.
Any place is dreary
Without my watch and you.

                LANGSTON HUGHES

Rhyme is part of the ballad writer's standard equipment, a fact
deriving originally from its value as an aid to memory but still working
in print to stress important words. Stanzas that rhyme abcb (as "Could
Be" does) are perhaps most common, but the ballad's rule is flexibility.
The ballad "Jesse James" uses internal rhymes—rhyming words in the
middle as well as at the ends of lines—to underline key words in its
insistent lament:

        Jesse had a wife to mourn for his life,
          Three children, they were brave;
        But the dirty little coward who shot Mr. Howard
          Has laid Jesse James in his grave.

Response 24

As our selections indicate, sudden death and misfortune in love are
common ballad subjects, as indeed they are in all poetry. Yet, how-
ever common these subjects are, they still can be endlessly varied.
Langston Hughes' treatment of the forlorn lover, for example, is
comic and refreshing, far from the usual stylized weeping.

Write a ballad of your own, patterning your rhymes and rhythms on
"Could Be" or "Bonnie George Campbell." Make your poem as
specific as they are; a ballad is always about a particular character
(Jesse James, not bandits generally) in a particular situation (the
occasion of Jesse James' death). Focus sharply on a crucial moment in
someone's life—your own or that of someone you've seen, perhaps a
public figure. Try to bring your ballad up to date by writing on a
contemporary situation.

Like the ballad, the sonnet form can be varied in keeping with the wishes of individual poets and the inherent logic of particular subjects. The form was supposedly invented by the Italian poet Petrarch and introduced into England during the sixteenth century, when it became extremely popular and was used by many poets, among them Shakespeare. The "rules" that the sonnet be fourteen lines long and in iambic pentameter generally hold true, but there are two basic models for the arrangement of rhymes. Look at the rhymes and the stanza divisions of the following examples.

ON THE GRASSHOPPER AND CRICKET

The poetry of earth is never dead:
   When all the birds are faint with the hot sun,
   And hide in cooling trees, a voice will run
From hedge to hedge about the new-mown mead;
That is the Grasshopper's—he takes the lead
   In summer luxury,—he has never done
   With his delights; for when tired out with fun
He rests at ease beneath some pleasant weed.
The poetry of earth is ceasing never:
   On a lone winter evening, when the frost   10
     Has wrought a silence, from the stove there shrills
The Cricket's song, in warmth increasing ever,
   And seems to one in drowsiness half lost,
     The Grasshopper's among some grassy hills.

JOHN KEATS

SONNET 73

That time of year thou mayst in me behold
When yellow leaves, or none, or few, do hang
Upon those boughs which shake against the cold,
Bare ruined choirs where late the sweet birds sang.
In me thou seest the twilight of such day
As after sunset fadeth in the west,
Which by and by black night doth take away,
Death's second self, that seals up all in rest.

In me thou seest the glowing of such fire
That on the ashes of his youth doth lie,   10
As the deathbed whereon it must expire,
Consumed with that which it was nourished by.
  This thou perceiv'st, which makes thy love more strong,
  To love that well which thou must leave ere long.

WILLIAM SHAKESPEARE

"On the Grasshopper and Cricket" is an Italian (or Petrarchan) sonnet. It is divided into a group of eight lines (the octave) and another of six lines (the sestet), rhyming abbaabba cdecde. (This pattern is a common one but not invariable.) Shakespeare's sonnet rhymes abab cdcd efef gg—three four-line stanzas (here printed as a solid block) and a concluding couplet. This pattern is called the English, or the Shakespearean, sonnet.

Each of these two forms seems to have certain inherent possibilities for ordering its subject matter. The two uneven parts of the Italian sonnet can easily frame such common sequences of thought as question-and-answer, cause-and-effect, problem-and-solution. Keats uses the form to provide two complementary proofs in support of his generalization that "the poetry of earth is never dead." The grasshopper, active in the summer heat, and the cricket, standing for ongoing life in the dead of winter, are the two halves that make up the wholeness of the year. The English sonnet, with its three equal line groups and concluding couplet, invites the poet to pile up evidence and provide a final summary, comment, or generalization. In "Sonnet 73" Shakespeare compares his age (in a poetic pose, he was in fact a comparatively young man when he wrote the poem) first to a tree in autumn, next to twilight, finally to a dying fire; he then concludes that the lover's passion is only intensified by the inevitability of death.

The danger of this sort of discussion is that it runs the risk of making the sonnet seem like a very cut-and-dried affair indeed. Perhaps "On the Grasshopper and Cricket" and "Sonnet 73," beautiful as they are for some readers, seem frighteningly perfect and remote to others. For contrast, let us look at some modern sonnets, beginning with one by Edna St. Vincent Millay from "Sonnets from an Ungrafted Tree."

SONNET 16

The doctor asked her what she wanted done
With him, that could not lie there many days.

And she was shocked to see how life goes on
Even after death, in irritating ways;
And mused how if he had not died at all
'Twould have been easier—then there need not be
The stiff disorder of a funeral
Everywhere, and the hideous industry,
And crowds of people calling her by name
And questioning her, she'd never seen before,   10
But only watching by his bed once more
And sitting silent if a knocking came . . .
She said at length, feeling the doctor's eyes,
"I don't know what you do exactly when a person dies."

EDNA ST. VINCENT MILLAY

Here the poet uses the English rhyme pattern but does not break the poem into stanzas; instead the lines follow the prose wanderings of the woman's mind as she tries to grasp what is happening and what she herself is called upon to do. The final line, in which she sums up her confusion for the doctor, has seven feet instead of the usual five, a rhythmic awkwardness that betrays her shock and uncertainty. Both love and nature, Shakespeare's and Keats' subjects, are present here, but the crude question about what to do with the beloved's corpse seems distinctively modern.

This expansion of the sonnet's traditional subject matter keeps pace with variations in its possible forms; changes of both kinds are evident in the two following examples.

OLD MEN AND OLD WOMEN GOING HOME ON THE STREET CAR

Carrying their packages of groceries in particular
With books under their arms that maybe they will read
And possibly understand, old women lead
Their weaker selves up to front of the car.

And old men who for thirty years have sat at desks
Survey them harmlessly.
                        They regard each other
As forgotten sister looks at forgotten brother
On their way between two easily remembered tasks
And that is positively all there is to it.

But it was not that way thirty years ago!   10
Before desks and counters had tired their backs and feet,

When life for them was a bowl of odorous fruit
That they might take their pick of, then turn and go
Saying, "This tastes so good!" or, "This smells so sweet!"

MERRILL MOORE

SMELL!

Oh strong ridged and deeply hollowed
nose of mine! what will you not be smelling?
What tactless asses we are, you and I, boney nose.
always indiscriminate, always unashamed,
and now it is the souring flowers of the bedraggled
poplars: a festering pulp on the wet earth
beneath them. With what deep thirst
we quicken our desires
to that rank odor of a passing springtime!
Can you not be decent? Can you not reserve your ardors   10
for something less unlovely? What girl will care
for us, do you think, if we continue in these ways?
Must you taste everything? Must you know everything?
Must you have a part in everything?

WILLIAM CARLOS WILLIAMS

Merrill Moore's sonnet uses an abbacddcefgefg rhyme scheme, but the way the lines are arranged conceals rather than reveals the sonnet form. Used this way, the sonnet becomes a structuring device that forces the poet to condense his meaning within a circumscribed space but plays down the tendency of a familiar form to call attention to itself. "Smell" complies only with the rule that the sonnet should be fourteen lines long. The poem is as bumptious and assertive as the nose it addresses, and seemingly as wayward, but it does make unobtrusive use of the sonnet form's potential by phrasing the last two lines as a series of questions which summarize all that has gone before. They even rhyme exactly, for the first and only rhyme in the poem.

Most of the varied new uses of the sonnet can be discovered at work in the next poem.

AUNT HELEN

Miss Helen Slingsby was my maiden aunt,
And lived in a small house near a fashionable square
Cared for by servants to the number of four.
Now when she died there was silence in heaven
And silence at her end of the street.
The shutters were drawn and the undertaker wiped his feet—
He was aware that this sort of thing had occurred before.
The dogs were handsomely provided for,
But shortly afterwards the parrot died too.
The Dresden clock continued ticking on the mantlepiece,   10
And the footman sat upon the dining-table
Holding the second housemaid on his knees—
Who had always been so careful while her mistress lived.

T. S. ELIOT

The rhymes—themselves not always perfect—do not occur in an order, but they are not quite random either: abbcddbbefgfh. It is as if an old order is being imperfectly recalled but efforts to achieve it consistently fail. The rhymes, in fact, reflect both the sterile order of Miss Helen Slingsby's life and its quick dispersal after her death. There are only thirteen lines in the poem; and the thirteenth, and final, line has six and a half trochaic—not, as we would expect, iambic—feet. Furthermore, its last word, "lived," rhymes with nothing that precedes it. Our expectation of a sonnet's being resolved at the end is thwarted, just as in the poem no one comes in to scold the housemaid and restore Miss Slingsby's decorum.

T. S. Eliot was exceptionally familiar with the history of poetry, and he may have seen a justification for his own experiments in those of such earlier poets as the Elizabethan, Fulke Greville, whose sonnets range from ten to thirty lines, or the nineteenth-century writer George Meredith, whose "Modern Love" sequence is made up of sonnets sixteen lines long. In any case, when Eliot "uses" the sonnet form by altering it almost out of recognition, he succeeds in mirroring a social order altered even more greatly. By doing so, he shows how flexible the sonnet can be.

Response 25

Pick out one of the poems which you have written for an earlier Response, not necessarily in this chapter, and which you now feel would benefit from a tighter structure. Rewrite it in accordance with some fixed pattern, perhaps a variation on the sonnet, and compare your two versions with those of other students.

*Poems
to read and discuss*

DO NOT GO GENTLE INTO THAT GOOD NIGHT

Do not go gentle into that good night,
Old age should burn and rave at close of day;
Rage, rage against the dying of the light.

Though wise men at their end know dark is right,
Because their words had forked no lightning they
Do not go gentle into that good night.

Good men, the last wave by, crying how bright
Their frail deeds might have danced in a green bay,
Rage, rage against the dying of the light.

Wild men who caught and sang the sun in flight,   10
And learn, too late, they grieved it on its way,
Do not go gentle into that good night.

Grave men, near death, who see with blinding sight
Blind eyes could blaze like meteors and be gay,
Rage, rage against the dying of the light.

And you, my father, there on the sad height,
Curse, bless, me now with your fierce tears, I pray.
Do not go gentle into that good night.
Rage, rage against the dying of the light.

                                        DYLAN THOMAS

from HALLELUJAH, ANYWAY

KENNETH PATCHEN

THE MENAGERIE AT VERSAILLES IN 1775

Taken verbatim from a notebook kept by
Dr. Samuel Johnson

Cygnets dark; their black feet;
on the ground; tame.
Halcyons, or gulls.
Stag and hind, small.
Aviary, very large: the net, wire.
Black stag of China, small.

Rhinoceros, the horn broken
and pared away, which, I suppose,
will grow; the basis, I think,
four inches 'cross; the skin   10
folds like loose cloth doubled over his body
and 'cross his hips: a vast animal,
though young; as big, perhaps,
as four oxen.

        The young elephant,
with his tusks just appearing.
The brown bear put out his paws.
All very tame. The lion.
The tigers I did not well view.
The camel, or dromedary with two bunches
called the Huguin, taller than any horse.   20
Two camels with one bunch.

Among the birds was a pelican,
who being let out, went
to a fountain, and swam
about to catch fish. His feet
well webbed: he dipped his head,
and turned his long bill sidewise.

                    JOHN UPDIKE

THE EDUCATORS

In their
limousines the

teachers come: by
hundreds. O the
square is
blackened with dark suits, with grave
scholastic faces. They
wait to be summoned.
　　　　　　　　These are the
educators, the
father-figures. O you could   10
warm with love for the firm lips, the
responsible foreheads. Their
ties are strongly set, between their collars. They
pass with dignity the exasperation of waiting.

A
bell rings. They turn. On the
wide steps my
dwarf is standing, both hands raised. He
cackles with laughter. Welcome, he cries, welcome
to our elaborate Palace. It is indeed. He   20
is tumbling in cartwheels over the steps. The
teachers turn to each other their grave faces.

With
a single grab they have him up by the shoulders. They
dismantle him. Limbs, O
limbs and delicate organs, limbs and
guts, eyes, the tongue, the
lobes of the brain, glands; tonsils, several
eyes, limbs, the tongue,
a kidney, pants, livers, more   30
kidneys, limbs, the tongue
pass from hand to hand, in their serious hands. He is
utterly gone. Wide
crumbling steps.

They
return to their cars. They
drive off smoothly, without disorder;
watching the road.

　　　　　　　　　　　D. M. BLACK

MASTER CHARGE BLUES

its wednesday night baby
and i'm all alone
wednesday night baby
and i'm all alone
sitting with myself
waiting for the telephone

wanted you baby
but you said you had to go
wanted you yeah
but you said you had to go   10
called your best friend
but he can't come 'cross no more

did you ever go to bed
at the end of a busy day
look over and see the smooth
where your hump usta lay
feminine odor and no reason why
i said feminine odor and no reason why
asked the lord to help me
he shook his head "not i"   20

but i'm a modern woman baby
ain't gonna let this get me down
i'm a modern woman
ain't gonna let this get me down
gonna take my master charge
and get everything in town

                              NIKKI GIOVANNI

SONNET 45

Care-charmer sleep, son of the sable night,
Brother to death, in silent darkness born;
Relieve my languish, and restore the light,
With dark forgetting of my cares return.
And let the day be time enough to mourn
The shipwreck of my ill-adventured youth;

Let waking eyes suffice to wail their scorn,
Without the torment of the night's untruth.
Cease dreams, th' images of day desires,
To model forth the passions of the morrow;   10
Never let rising sun approve you liars,
To add more grief to aggravate my sorrow.
   Still let me sleep, embracing clouds in vain;
   And never wake to feel the day's disdain.

                                SAMUEL DANIEL

FOR A HIGH-SCHOOL COMMENCEMENT

Did you suppose that now you were set free?—
That now, the ritual complete, you met
The world at last?—Oh, children, do you know,
Now, the sense of victory past and gain complete?
   (Children, you are very little,
   And your bones are very brittle:
   If you would grow tall and stately
   You must learn to walk sedately.)

Here and now you are honored and given the unction
Of your elders' tainted wisdom: you are told   10
That this old world, so sadly smirched by us,
Falls now to youth to heal—"therefore be bold!"
   (Children, you are very witless,
   And your little hearts quite pitiless:
   If you would learn to walk erectly
   You must feel some pain directly.)

Your party clothes are underneath your gowns
And you grow fretful, waiting for dismissal,
While your families grow tearful over Elgar
And temporarily take known lies for gospel.   20
   (Children, you are very restless,
   And your spirits very selfish:
   If you ever would be giving
   You must quickly do some living.)

But this address by me is scarcely different
From that of other graduation speakers:
And you who listen meet no less deception
Than if I told you you must all be "leaders."
    (Children, you are very common
    And your vices very human: 30
    If you would be called mature
    All you must do is endure.)

                    JUDITH K. MOORE

DREAMS OF THE ANIMALS

Mostly the animals dream
of other animals   each
according to its kind

      (though certain mice and small rodents
      have nightmares of a huge pink
      shape with five claws descending)

:moles dream of darkness and delicate
mole smells

frogs dream of green and golden
frogs   10
sparkling like wet suns
among the lilies

red and black
striped fish, their eyes open
have red and black striped
dreams   defence, attack, meaningful
patterns

birds dream of territories
enclosed by singing.

Sometimes the animals dream of evil   20
in the form of soap and metal
but mostly the animals dream
of other animals.

There are exceptions:

the silver fox in the roadside zoo
dreams of digging out
and of baby foxes, their necks bitten

the caged armadillo
near the train
station, which runs   30
all day in figure eights
its piglet feet pattering,
no longer dreams
but is insane when waking;

the iguana
in the petshop window on St Catherine Street
crested, royal-eyed, ruling
its kingdom of water-dish and sawdust

dreams of sawdust.

MARGARET ATWOOD

CARENTAN O CARENTAN

Trees in the old days used to stand
And shape a shady lane
Where lovers wandered hand in hand
Who came from Carentan.

This was the shining green canal
Where we came two by two
Walking at combat-interval.
Such trees we never knew.

The day was early June, the ground
Was soft and bright with dew.   10
Far away the guns did sound,
But here the sky was blue.

The sky was blue, but there a smoke
Hung still above the sea
Where the ships together spoke
To towns we could not see.

Could you have seen us through a glass
You would have said a walk
Of farmers out to turn the grass,
Each with his own hay-fork.   20

The watchers in their leopard suits
Waited till it was time,
And aimed between the belt and boot
And let the barrel climb.

I must lie down at once, there is
A hammer at my knee.
And call it death or cowardice,
Don't count again on me.

Everything's all right, Mother,
Everyone gets the same   30
At one time or another.
It's all in the game.

I never strolled, nor ever shall,
Down such a leafy lane.
I never drank in a canal,
Nor ever shall again.

There is a whistling in the leaves
And it is not the wind,
The twigs are falling from the knives
That cut men to the ground.   40

Tell me, Master-Sergeant,
The way to turn and shoot.
But the Sergeant's silent
That taught me how to do it.

O Captain, show us quickly
Our place upon the map.
But the Captain's sickly
And taking a long nap.

Lieutenant, what's my duty,
My place in the platoon? 50
He too's a sleeping beauty,
Charmed by that strange tune.

Carentan O Carentan
Before we met with you
We never yet had lost a man
Or known what death could do.

LOUIS SIMPSON

THE BALLAD OF RUDOLPH REED

Rudolph Reed was oaken.
His wife was oaken too.
And his two good girls and his good little man
Oakened as they grew.

"I am not hungry for berries.
I am not hungry for bread.
But hungry hungry for a house
Where at night a man in bed

"May never hear the plaster
Stir as if in pain. 10
May never hear the roaches
Falling like fat rain.

"Where never wife and children need
Go blinking through the gloom.
Where every room of many rooms
Will be full of room.

"Oh my home may have its east or west
Or north or south behind it.
All I know is I shall know it,
And fight for it when I find it." 20

It was in a street of bitter white
That he made his application.
For Rudolph Reed was oakener
Than others in the nation.

The agent's steep and steady stare
Corroded to a grin.
Why, you black old, tough old hell of a man,
Move your family in!

Nary a grin grinned Rudolph Reed,
Nary a curse cursed he,   30
But moved in his House. With his dark little wife,
And his dark little children three.

A neighbor would *look,* with a yawning eye
That squeezed into a slit.
But the Rudolph Reeds and the children three
Were too joyous to notice it.

For were they not firm in a home of their own
With windows everywhere
And a beautiful banistered stair
And a front yard for flowers and a back yard for grass?   40

The first night, a rock, big as two fists.
The second, a rock big as three.
But nary a curse cursed Rudolph Reed.
(Though oaken as man could be.)

The third night, a silvery ring of glass.
Patience ached to endure.
But he looked, and lo! small Mabel's blood
Was staining her gaze so pure.

Then up did rise our Rudolph Reed
And pressed the hand of his wife,   50
And went to the door with a thirty-four
And a beastly butcher knife.

He ran like a mad thing into the night.
And the words in his mouth were stinking.
By the time he had hurt his first white man
He was no longer thinking.

By the time he had hurt his fourth white man
Rudolph Reed was dead.
His neighbors gathered and kicked his corpse.
"Nigger—" his neighbors said.   60

Small Mabel whimpered all night long,
For calling herself the cause.
Her oak-eyed mother did no thing
But change the bloody gauze.

GWENDOLYN BROOKS

THE FEAR

A lantern-light from deeper in the barn
Shone on a man and woman in the door
And threw their lurching shadows on a house
Nearby, all dark in every glossy window.
A horse's hoof pawed once the hollow floor,
And the back of the gig they stood beside
Moved in a little. The man grasped a wheel.
The woman spoke out sharply, "Whoa, stand still!—
I saw it just as plain as a white plate,"
She said, "as the light on the dashboard ran   10
Along the bushes at the roadside—a man's face.
You *must* have seen it too."
                              "I didn't see it.
Are you sure——"
                "Yes, I'm sure!"
                                "—it was a face?"

"Joel, I'll have to look. I can't go in,
I can't, and leave a thing like that unsettled.
Doors locked and curtains drawn will make no difference.
I always have felt strange when we came home
To the dark house after so long an absence,
And the key rattled loudly into place
Seemed to warn someone to be getting out   20
At one door as we entered at another.
What if I'm right, and someone all the time—
Don't hold my arm!"
                    "I say it's someone passing."

"You speak as if this were a traveled road.
You forget where we are. What is beyond
That he'd be going to or coming from
At such an hour of night, and on foot too?
What was he standing still for in the bushes?"

"It's not so very late—it's only dark.
There's more in it than you're inclined to say.   30
Did he look like——?"
                        "He looked like anyone.
I'll never rest tonight unless I know.
Give me the lantern."
                        "You don't want the lantern."

She pushed past him and got it for herself.

"You're not to come," she said. "This is my business.
If the time's come to face it, I'm the one
To put it the right way. He'd never dare—
Listen! He kicked a stone. Hear that, hear that!
He's coming towards us. Joel, *go* in—please.
Hark!—I don't hear him now. But please go in."   40

"In the first place you can't make me believe it's——"

"It is—or someone else he's sent to watch.
And now's the time to have it out with him
While we know definitely where he is.
Let him get off and he'll be everywhere
Around us, looking out of trees and bushes
Till I shan't dare to set a foot outdoors.
And I can't stand it. Joel, let me go!"

"But it's nonsense to think he'd care enough."

"You mean you couldn't understand his caring.   50
Oh, but you see he hadn't had enough—
Joel, I won't—I won't—I promise you.
We mustn't say hard things. You mustn't either."

"I'll be the one, if anybody goes!
But you give him the advantage with this light.
What couldn't he do to us standing here!
And if to see was what he wanted, why,
He has seen all there was to see and gone."

He appeared to forget to keep his hold,
But advanced with her as she crossed the grass.   60

"What do you want?" she cried to all the dark.
She stretched up tall to overlook the light
That hung in both hands, hot against her skirt.

"There's no one; so you're wrong," he said.
                                        "There is.—
What do you want?" she cried, and then herself
Was startled when an answer really came.

"Nothing." It came from well along the road.

She reached a hand to Joel for support:
The smell of scorching woolen made her faint.
"What are you doing round this house at night?"   70

"Nothing." A pause: there seemed no more to say.

And then the voice again: "You seem afraid.
I saw by the way you whipped up the horse.
I'll just come forward in the lantern-light
And let you see."
                    "Yes, do.—Joel, go back!"
She stood her ground against the noisy steps
That came on, but her body rocked a little.

"You see," the voice said.
                            "Oh." She looked and looked.

"You don't see—I've a child here by the hand.
A robber wouldn't have his family with him."   80

"What's a child doing at this time of night——?"

"Out walking. Every child should have the memory
Of at least one long-after-bedtime walk.
What, son?"
                "Then I should think you'd try to find
Somewhere to walk——"

                        "The highway, as it happens—
We're stopping for the fortnight down at Dean's."

"But if that's all—Joel—you realize—
You won't think anything. You understand?
You understand that we have to be careful.
This is a very, very lonely place.—   90
Joel!" She spoke as if she couldn't turn.
The swinging lantern lengthened to the ground,
It touched, it struck, it clattered and went out.

ROBERT FROST

SONNET 12

I did but prompt the age to quit their clogs
    By the known rules of ancient liberty,
    When straight a barbarous noise environs me
    Of owls and cuckoos, asses, apes, and dogs;
As when those hinds that were transformed to frogs
    Railed at Latona's twin-born progeny,
    Which after held the sun and moon in fee.
    But this is got by casting pearl to hogs,

That bawl for freedom in their senseless mood,
    And still revolt when truth would set them free.   10
    License they mean when they cry liberty;
For who loves that must first be wise and good:
    But from that mark how far they rove we see,
    For all this waste of wealth and loss of blood.

JOHN MILTON

WE WEAR THE MASK

We wear the mask that grins and lies,
It hides our cheeks and shades our eyes,—
This debt we pay to human guile;
With torn and bleeding hearts we smile,
And mouth with myriad subtleties.

Why should the world be overwise,
In counting all our tears and sighs?
Nay, let them only see us, while
    We wear the mask.

We smile, but O great Christ, our cries   10
To Thee from tortured souls arise.
We sing, but oh, the clay is vile
Beneath our feet, and long the mile;
But let the world dream otherwise,
    We wear the mask.

PAUL LAURENCE DUNBAR

DEATH THE LEVELLER

The glories of our blood and state,
    are shadows, not substantial things,
There is no armour against fate,
    Death lays his icy hand on Kings,
            Scepter and Crown,
            Must tumble down,
And in the dust be equal made,
With the poor crooked sithe and spade.

Some men with swords may reap the field,
　　and plant fresh laurels where they kill,　　　　10
But their strong nerves at last must yield,
　　They tame but one another still;
　　　　　　Early or late,
　　　　　　They stoop to fate,
And must give up their murmuring breath,
When they pale Captives creep to death.

The Garlands wither on your brow,
　　Then boast no more your mighty deeds,
Upon Deaths purple Altar now,
　　See where the Victor-victim bleeds,　　　　20
　　　　　　Your heads must come,
　　　　　　To the cold Tomb,
Onely the actions of the just
Smell sweet, and blossom in their dust.

　　　　　　　　　JAMES SHIRLEY

UNWANTED

The poster with my picture on it
Is hanging on the bulletin board in the Post Office.

I stand by it hoping to be recognized
Posing first full face and then profile

But everybody passes by and I have to admit
The photograph was taken some years ago.

I was unwanted then and I'm unwanted now
Ah guess ah'll go up echo mountain and crah.

I wish someone would find my fingerprints somewhere
Maybe on a corpse and say, You're it.　　　　10

Description: Male, or reasonably so
White, but not lily-white and usually deep-red

Thirty-fivish, and looks it lately
Five-feet-nine and one-hundred-thirty pounds: no physique

Black hair going gray, hairline receding fast
What used to be curly, now fuzzy

Brown eyes starey under beetling brow
Mole on chin, probably will become a wen

It is perfectly obvious that he was not popular at school
No good at baseball, and wet his bed.   20

His aliases tell his history: Dumbell, Good-for-nothing,
Jewboy, Fieldinsky, Skinny, Fierce Face, Greaseball, Sissy.

Warning: This man is not dangerous, answers to any name
Responds to love, don't call him or he will come.

EDWARD FIELD

THE HOSPITAL IN WINTER

A dark bell leadens the hour,
    the three-o'clock
light falls amber across a tower.

Below, green-railed within a wall
    of coral brick,
stretches the borough hospital

monstrous with smells that cover death,
    white gauze tongues,
cold-water-pipes of pain, glass breath,

porcelain, blood, black rubber tires   10
    and in the yards
plane trees and slant telephone wires.

On benches squat the afraid and cold
    hour after hour.
Chains of windows snarl with gold.

Far off, beyond the engine-sheds,
    motionless trucks
grow ponderous, their rotting reds

deepening towards night; from windows
    bathrobed men   20
watch the horizon flare as the light goes.

Smoke whispers across the town,
    high panes are bleak;
pink of coral sinks to brown;
a dark bell brings the dark down.

ROY FISHER

BIRTHDAY POEM

First light of day in Mississippi
son of laborer & of house wife
it says so on the official photostat
not son of fisherman & child fugitive
from cotton fields & potato patches
from sugarcane chickens & well-water
from kerosene lamps & watermelons
mules named jack or jenny & wagonwheels,

years of meaningless farm work
work Work Work WORK *WORK*—
"Papa pull you outta school bout March
to stay on the place & work the crop"
—her own earliest knowledge
of human hopelessness & waste

She carried me around nine months
inside her fifteen year old self
before here I sit numbering it all

How I got from then to now
is the mystery that could fill a whole library
much less an arbitrary stanza   20

But of course you already know about that
from your own random suffering
& sudden inexplicable bliss

AL YOUNG

SESTINA

September rain falls on the house.
In the failing light, the old grandmother
sits in the kitchen with the child
beside the Little Marvel Stove,
reading the jokes from the almanac,
laughing and talking to hide her tears.

She thinks that her equinoctial tears
and the rain that beats on the roof of the house
were both foretold by the almanac,
but only known to a grandmother.   10
The iron kettle sings on the stove.
She cuts some bread and says to the child,

It's time for tea now; but the child
is watching the teakettle's small hard tears
dance like mad on the hot black stove,
the way the rain must dance on the house.
Tidying up, the old grandmother
hangs up the clever almanac

on its string. Birdlike, the almanac
hovers half open above the child,   20
hovers above the old grandmother
and her teacup full of dark brown tears.
She shivers and says she thinks the house
feels chilly, and puts more wood in the stove.

It was to be, says the Marvel Stove.
I know what I know, says the almanac.
With crayons the child draws a rigid house
and a winding pathway. Then the child
puts in a man with buttons like tears
and shows it proudly to the grandmother.   30

But secretly, while the grandmother
busies herself about the stove,
the little moons fall down like tears
from between the pages of the almanac
into the flower bed the child
has carefully placed in the front of the house.

Time to plant tears, says the almanac.
The grandmother sings to the marvellous stove
and the child draws another inscrutable house.

ELIZABETH BISHOP

WE ASSUME

On the Death of Our Son, Reuben Masai Harper

We assume
that in 28 hours,
lived in a collapsible isolette,
you learned to accept pure oxygen
as the natural sky;
the scant shallow breaths
that filled those hours
cannot, did not make you fly—
but dreams were there
like crooked palmprints on   10
the twin-thick windows of the nursery—
in the glands of your mother.

We assume
the sterile hands
drank chemicals in and out
from lungs opaque with mucus,
pumped your stomach,
eeked the bicarbonate in
crooked, green-winged veins,
out in a plastic mask;   20

A woman who'd lost her first son
consoled us with an angel gone ahead
to pray for our family—
gone into that sky
seeking oxygen,
gone into autopsy,
a fine brown powdered sugar,
a disposable cremation:

We assume
you did not know we loved you.   30

MICHAEL HARPER

LYDIA SHERMAN IS PLAGUED WITH RATS

Lydia Sherman is plagued with rats.
Lydia has no faith in cats.
So Lydia buys some arsenic,
And then her husband he gets sick;
And then her husband, he does die,
And Lydia's neighbors wonder why.

Lydia moves, but still has rats;
And still she puts no faith in cats;
So again she buys some arsenic,
This time her children, they get sick,   10
This time her children, they do die,
And Lydia's neighbors wonder why.

Lydia lies in Wethersfield jail,
And loudly she does moan and wail.
She blames her fate on a plague of rats;
She blames the laziness of cats.
But her neighbors' questions she can't deny—
So Lydia now in prison must lie.

ANONYMOUS

MY FRIEND, WENDELL BERRY

My friend, Wendell Berry
bought a pocket watch
like this one:

for 25¢
off the back of a truck in San Francisco.
He was real excited and happy
about his shrewd deal.
I, a sophisticated midwesterner
with an $80
watch   10
like this one

given to me by my mother
was simply unimpressed
and a little amused.

You see, Wendell is from
a couple of miles
below the Ohio River
and I'm from several
miles above the Ohio River
in the lap of culture.   20

Well, yesterday, my $80 watch
broke
and Wendell offered
to sell me his watch
for 50¢
—that would be a 100% profit!
So I went to
this discount place, Baz'r
and bought a watch
like this one: 30

for $3.66. Obviously a better watch
than Wendell's.
But I ain't never
talking to Mr. Wendell Berry again.

WILLIAM J. HARRIS

MISS GEE

Let me tell you a little story
    About Miss Edith Gee;
She lived in Clevedon Terrace
    At Number 83.

She'd a slight squint in her left eye,
    Her lips they were thin and small,
She had narrow sloping shoulders
    And she had no bust at all.

She'd a velvet hat with trimmings,
    And a dark grey serge costume;   10
She lived in Clevedon Terrace
    In a small bed-sitting room.

She'd a purple mac for wet days,
  A green umbrella too to take,
She'd a bicycle with shopping basket
  And a harsh back-pedal brake.

The Church of Saint Aloysius
  Was not so very far;
She did a lot of knitting,
  Knitting for that Church Bazaar.   20

Miss Gee looked up at the starlight
  And said, 'Does anyone care
That I live in Clevedon Terrace
  On one hundred pounds a year?'

She dreamed a dream one evening
  That she was the Queen of France
And the Vicar of Saint Aloysius
  Asked Her Majesty to dance.

But a storm blew down the palace,
  She was biking through a field of corn,   30
And a bull with the face of the Vicar
  Was charging with lowered horn.

She could feel his hot breath behind her,
  He was going to overtake;
And the bicycle went slower and slower
  Because of that back-pedal brake.

Summer made the trees a picture,
  Winter made them a wreck;
She bicycled to the evening service
  With her clothes buttoned up to her neck.   40

She passed by the loving couples,
  She turned her head away;
She passed by the loving couples
  And they didn't ask her to stay.

Miss Gee sat down in the side-aisle,
  She heard the organ play;
And the choir it sang so sweetly
  At the ending of the day,

Miss Gee knelt down in the side-aisle,
   She knelt down on her knees;   50
'Lead me not into temptation
   But make me a good girl, please.'

The days and nights went by her
   Like waves round a Cornish wreck;
She bicycled down to the doctor
   With her clothes buttoned up to her neck.

She bicycled down to the doctor,
   And rang the surgery bell;
'O, doctor, I've a pain inside me,
   And I don't feel very well.'   60

Doctor Thomas looked her over,
   And then he looked some more;
Walked over to his wash-basin,
   Said, 'Why didn't you come before?'

Doctor Thomas sat over his dinner,
   Though his wife was waiting to ring,
Rolling his bread into pellets;
   Said, 'Cancer's a funny thing.

'Nobody knows what the cause is,
   Though some pretend they do;   70
It's like some hidden assassin
   Waiting to strike at you.

'Childless women get it,
   And men when they retire;
It's as if there had to be some outlet
   For their foiled creative fire.'

His wife she rang for the servant,
   Said, 'Don't be so morbid, dear';
He said: 'I saw Miss Gee this evening
   And she's a goner, I fear.'   80

They took Miss Gee to the hospital,
   She lay there a total wreck,

Lay in the ward for women
    With the bedclothes right up to her neck.

They laid her on the table,
    The students began to laugh;
And Mr. Rose the surgeon
    He cut Miss Gee in half.

Mr. Rose he turned to his students,
    Said, 'Gentlemen, if you please,   90
We seldom see a sarcoma
    As far advanced as this.'

They took her off the table,
    They wheeled away Miss Gee
Down to another department
    Where they study Anatomy.

They hung her from the ceiling,
    Yes, they hung up Miss Gee;
And a couple of Oxford Groupers
    Carefully dissected her knee.   100

W. H. AUDEN

BUFFALO BILL'S DEFUNCT

Buffalo Bill's
defunct
        who used to
        ride a watersmooth-silver
                                stallion
and break onetwothreefourfive pigeonsjustlikethat
                                        Jesus

he was a handsome man
                and what i want to know is
how do you like your blueeyed boy   10
Mister Death

e. e. cummings

SHAPES

THE OWL AND THE PUSSY-CAT

I

The Owl and the Pussy-Cat went to sea
  In a beautiful pea-green boat,
They took some honey, and plenty of money,
  Wrapped up in a five-pound note.
The Owl looked up to the stars above,
  And sang to a small guitar,
'O lovely Pussy! O Pussy, my love,
  What a beautiful Pussy you are,
    You are,
    You are!   10
What a beautiful Pussy you are!'

II

Pussy said to the Owl, 'You elegant fowl!
  How charmingly sweet you sing!
O let us be married! too long we have tarried,
  But what shall we do for a ring?'
They sailed away for a year and a day,
  To the land where the Bong-tree grows,
And there in a wood a Piggy-wig stood,
  With a ring at the end of his nose,
    His nose,   20
    His nose,
  With a ring at the end of his nose.

III

'Dear Pig, are you willing to sell for one shilling
  Your ring?' Said the Piggy, 'I will.'
So they took it away, and were married next day
  By the Turkey who lives on the hill.
They dinèd on mince, and slices of quince,
  Which they ate with a runcible spoon;
And hand in hand, on the edge of the sand,
  They danced by the light of the moon,   30
    The moon,
    The moon,
  They danced by the light of the moon.

EDWARD LEAR

6
Expectations and Surprises

We've mentioned several times that the poet creates expectations in his reader, for example, with rhyme and rhythm. These expectations have sometimes been fulfilled, sometimes not, all for the purpose of evoking various reactions at specific points in the poem. But whole poems occur in a context of expectations as well, a context of assumptions about language, about poetry, and about certain kinds of poems.

Response 26

Take our language. Is the language of poetry the same as the language you speak every day? Take each of the three words in one of the following groups and use it in a sentence (making a total of three sentences). Discuss with other students the differences in the sentences you write.

dawn	good-bye	regurgitate
morning	see you later	vomit
six A.M.	farewell	throw up

Words like "dawn" and "farewell," and especially "regurgitate" may strike you immediately as more formal; you probably find it more comfortable to use "morning" or "good-bye"—to use them, that is, familiarly, without self-consciousness. Many people, however, believe that the formal words are the right ones for poetry. They seem to have in mind, without having thought much about it, a number of words that they regard as especially suited to poetry, usually, words that would be rather embarrassing to use in daily speech. For an example of such elevated words in action, examine the following youthful poem by Tennyson.

THE SLEEPING BEAUTY

I

Year after year unto her feet,
   She lying on her couch alone,
Across the purpled coverlet,
   The maiden's jet-black hair has grown,
On either side her tranced form
   Forth streaming from a braid of pearl:
The slumbrous light is rich and warm,
   And moves not on the rounded curl.

II

The silk star-broider'd coverlid
   Unto her limbs itself doth mould   10
Languidly ever; and, amid
   Her full black ringlets downward roll'd,
Glows forth each softly-shadow'd arm
   With bracelets of the diamond bright:
Her constant beauty doth inform
   Stillness with love, and day with light.

III

She sleeps: her breathings are not heard
   In palace chambers far apart.
The fragrant tresses are not stirr'd
   That lie upon her charmed heart.   20
She sleeps: on either hand upswells
   The gold-fringed pillow lightly prest:
She sleeps, nor dreams, but ever dwells
   A perfect form in perfect rest.

           ALFRED, LORD TENNYSON

Whether or not you respond to the lush beauty of the picture Tennyson paints, few of you would use his language today. Not only words like "tranced," "slumbrous," "languidly," and "tresses," but even prepositions like "unto" and "amid" strike us as almost foreign. In addition, constructions like "forth streaming," "moves not," "the diamond bright," and "She sleeps, nor dreams" arrange words in a strange and unproselike order.

Before you decide that Tennyson is merely unrealistic and old-fashioned, look at a contemporary poem that concentrates as much on ugliness as Tennyson does on beauty.

NO GREAT MATTER

An ugly old man
with camel brown fingers
(lungs as black
as a coal town alley)
stepped from a doorway
onto the curb
beneath a sightless urine-yellow moon
and coughed just twice
before the sidewalk smashed his eyes out.

Forty minutes later,   10
after every banker's daughter
kissed the son of every lawyer
beneath every lemonade-mellow kiwanis club moon
in Grand Island Nebraska,
the police slithered up
and called for the wagon.

A frowsy old nag
with a mole on her eye
who fancied herself a senior whore,
hung both her chins   20
on the window ledge
and belched the national anthem,
and told the cops she never saw him sober.

DAVID LAWSON

At first glance David Lawson's poem seems to handle the English language as we all do. Phrases like "stepped from a doorway" or "forty minutes later" certainly are the stuff of prose narrative, even of newspaper reporting. But would most people, in speech (or in writing, outside of fiction), make the comparisons "camel brown fingers" or "lungs as black as a coal town alley"? Would they comment on the moon at all (beyond perhaps the bald statement that it was a moonlit night), much less set up the two versions of the same moon, on the one hand "sightless urine-yellow," and on the other "lemonade-mellow kiwanis club"?

Clearly, the issue of "poetic diction," of the words appropriate to poetry, is more complex than it at first seems. Poets and critics have argued about it for centuries. There are no easy answers. Is it equally impossible for David Lawson to write about "fragrant tresses" and for Tennyson to write about a "urine-yellow moon"? If so, then there is more involved than a mere choice of words. Choices of subject matter and attitude are also being made. Tennyson's search for perfect beauty led him to a romantic fairy tale, while David Lawson's view of reality forced him to face the ugliness and futility lit up by the "sightless urine-yellow moon." Since we are contemporaries of David Lawson and not of Tennyson, our expectations tend to be more readily fulfilled by "No Great Matter" than by "The Sleeping Beauty."

Differences between cultures (and between experiences within cultures) can affect poetry as much as the differences between Lawson's time and Tennyson's. Consider the distance of the following poem and then observe how every element in it has meaning in its own cultural context. The poem comes from the Ghost-Dance Religion, a religious revival that swept American Indian tribes late in the nineteenth century, when the hope of successful resistance to the white man's advance was becoming impossible to hold onto. Ghost-Dance poems—really songs—reported the trance visions of the religion's followers. The poem printed below, by emphasizing the return of the ancestors and the buffalo, sums up the Indian's dream of recovering his lost way of life. The eagle and the crow were regarded as sacred birds.

THE WHOLE WORLD IS COMING

The whole world is coming.
A nation is coming, a nation is coming,
The Eagle has brought the message to the tribe.
The father says so, the father says so.
Over the whole earth they are coming.
The buffalo are coming, the buffalo are coming,
The Crow has brought the message to the tribe,
The father says so, the father says so.

                        AMERICAN INDIAN, TRADITIONAL

The mixture of linguistic and moral expectations that we bring to poetry is especially clear in parody. In *The Waste Land,* T. S. Eliot parodied the following poem by Oliver Goldsmith, which first appeared in the year 1776, in his novel *The Vicar of Wakefield.*

SONG

When lovely woman stoops to folly,
    And finds too late that men betray,
What charm can sooth her melancholy,
    What art can wash her guilt away?

The only art her guilt to cover,
  To hide her shame from every eye,
To give repentance to her lover,
  And wring his bosom—is to die.

OLIVER GOLDSMITH

T. S. Eliot's parody appeared in 1922 and varied quite a bit from Goldsmith's poem.

When lovely woman stoops to folly and
Paces about her room again, alone,
She smoothes her hair with automatic hand,
And puts a record on the gramophone.

Eliot not only refrains from using such words as "shame" and "repentance," he also shows his "lovely woman" as concerned with trivial things and indifferent to moral judgments. He uses modern words like "automatic" and "gramophone" (nowadays you might want to use "stereo" or even "tape deck") because he wants to suggest a contemporary attitude radically different from Goldsmith's. Eliot makes fun of both the sentimental seriousness of Goldsmith's poem and the frivolity of modern women.

Part of the impact of Eliot's parody, of course, rests on the reader's recognition that a parody is intended. If the reader does not know Goldsmith's poem, much of what Eliot does will be missed. A very familiar source will make for successful parody, which we can demonstrate from Eve Merriam's book *The Inner-City Mother Goose.* If you know "I had a little nut tree, nothing would it bear/But a silver nutmeg and a golden pear;/ The King of Spain's daughter came to visit me,/ All on account of my little nut tree," you will immediately recognize

I had a little teevee,
Kept it over there,
Over by the window;
Now the place is bare.

The installment collector
Came to visit me,
And all for the sake of
My little teevee.

Response 27

Write a parody of one of the following poems; use modern language and present-day attitudes. In parody, you first decide on your readers' expectations, then play with them instead of fulfilling them. Invent a way to turn the expectations for one of the next three poems upside-down.

ON HIS SEVENTY-FIFTH BIRTHDAY

I strove with none; for none was worth my strife,
   Nature I loved, and next to Nature, Art;
I warmed both hands before the fire of life,
   It sinks, and I am ready to depart.

WALTER SAVAGE LANDOR

MY HEART LEAPS UP

My heart leaps up when I behold
   A rainbow in the sky:
So was it when my life began;
So is it now I am a man;
So be it when I shall grow old,
   Or let me die!
The Child is father of the Man;
And I could wish my days to be
Bound each to each by natural piety.

WILLIAM WORDSWORTH

THE INDIAN SERENADE

1

I arise from dreams of thee
In the first sweet sleep of night.
When the winds are breathing low,
And the stars are shining bright:
I arise from dreams of thee,
And a spirit in my feet
Hath led me—who knows how?
To thy chamber window, Sweet!

2

The wandering airs they faint
On the dark, the silent stream—   10
The Champak odors fail
Like sweet thoughts in a dream;
The nightingale's complaint,
It dies upon her heart—
As I must on thine,
Oh, beloved as thou art!

3

Oh lift me from the grass!
I die! I faint! I fail!
Let thy love in kisses rain
On my lips and eyelids pale.   20
My cheek is cold and white, alas!
My heart beats loud and fast—
Oh! press it to thine own again,
Where it will break at last.

PERCY BYSSHE SHELLEY

Entertaining as parody may be, you can find it working against you.
A straightforward love poem, for instance, may be open to parody,
but does anyone, however modern he thinks himself, want to deny
himself the use of poetry to express love? LeRoi Jones avoids the
clichés that have come to sound insincere. Instead, he focuses on a
detail that for him symbolizes his wife's whole character. An appar-
ent criticism serves as an expression of admiration.

FOR HETTIE

My wife is left-handed,
Which implies a fierce de-
termination. A complete other
worldliness. IT'S WIERD BABY
The way some folks
are always trying to be different.
A sin and a shame.

But then, she's been a bohemian
all her life . . . black stockings,
refusing to take orders. I sit   10
patiently, trying to tell her
what's right. TAKE THAT DAMM
PENCIL OUTTA THAT HAND. YOU'RE
RITING BACKWARDS and such. But,
to no avail. And it shows
in her work. Left-handed coffee,
left-handed eggs: when she comes
in at night . . . it's her left hand
offered for me to kiss. DAMM.

And now her belly droops over the seat.   20
They say it's a child. But
I ain't quite so sure.

                              LEROI JONES

The poem's title, "For Hettie," is conventional for a love poem, a poem *for* the beloved. Left-handedness seems a strange subject when you discover it in these surroundings, until you see it as the outward sign of Hettie's uniqueness, which Jones makes you see by his play-fully scolding tone. When this connection is made, you find yourself back in touch with the underlying formula that you probably expected to meet in the first place: "There's no one like my loved one." Expecta-tion is first aroused, then baffled, then finally satisfied in a new way.

Subjects such as love have always had much human interest. Anoth-er subject of obvious human interest is war, even though styles in poetry come and go. Consider, for example, the following two poems about dead soldiers.

ODE

Written in the Beginning of the Year 1746

How sleep the brave, who sink to rest,
By all their country's wishes bless'd!
When Spring, with dewy fingers cold,
Returns to deck their hallow'd mould,
She there shall dress a sweeter sod
Than Fancy's feet have ever trod.

By fairy hands their knell is rung;
By forms unseen their dirge is sung;
There Honour comes, a pilgrim gray,
To bless the turf that wraps their clay;   10
And Freedom shall a while repair,
To dwell a weeping hermit there!

                    WILLIAM COLLINS

ANTHEM FOR DOOMED YOUTH

What passing-bells for these who die as cattle?
    Only the monstrous anger of the guns.
Only the stuttering rifles' rapid rattle
    Can patter out their hasty orisons.
No mockeries for them from prayers or bells,
    Nor any voice of mourning save the choirs,—
The shrill, demented choirs of wailing shells;
    And bugles calling for them from sad shires.

What candles may be held to speed them all?
    Not in the hands of boys, but in their eyes   10
Shall shine the holy glimmers of good-byes.
    The pallor of girls' brows shall be their pall;
Their flowers the tenderness of silent minds,
And each slow dusk a drawing-down of blinds.

                    WILFRED OWEN

The use of Spring, Honour, and Freedom in Collins' poem conforms
to the poetic style of his age, but these words are not just quaint bits
of decoration. Honour as a pilgrim, Freedom as a hermit, even Spring

"with dewy fingers cold" (far from our conventional idea of spring), all suggest mourning and death. In their own way they intensify the deadness of the soldiers as strongly as do Wilfred Owen's references to guns, rifles, and shells. Owen, a young poet killed in World War I, refers ironically to the older poetic traditions that glamorized death in battle. In this poem he makes the sound of guns and rifles stand for mourning church bells and prayers for the dead; the chants we might expect to hear sung at a solemn memorial service are transformed into "the shrill, demented choirs of wailing shells." The formal trappings of ritual mourning become fused with the chaos of battle.

Like love and war, nature is also a subject we are used to thinking of as especially suited to poetry, and many of us also wonder how anyone can possibly say anything new and true about it. Here is a poem that makes an attempt.

SNOW

Smooths and burdens,
endangers, hardens.

Erases, revises.
Extemporizes

Vistas of lunar solitude.
Builds, embellishes a mood.

      ROBERT HAYDEN

If you examine the poem closely you find that its manner, a piling on of verbs and verb phrases, is as much a part of the meaning as the subject matter. Your expectation of full sentences and descriptive adjectives is not met. The reference to "lunar solitude" evokes our current knowledge of space travel, and is probably not a comparison that would have been made even ten years ago. These things make you look anew at the familiar subject of snow.

Response 28

Take one of the traditional themes—love, war, nature—and write a poem that presents your own insights on the subject. See what you can do to be both fresh and honest.

The variety of styles and languages in which poetry appears raises the problem of the reader's knowledge. As you have seen, you need to know an original source in order to appreciate a parody; similarly, you need to be aware of the tradition of solemn funeral poetry in order to recognize that Owen relocates that tradition among the noises of modern warfare in developing his ironies. It is this idea of tradition as something ongoing and constantly interacting with the present that makes it still hold the interest of modern readers. If "For Hettie" did not in the end satisfy an old expectation in a new way, the reader would be displeased with it. He would be either bored by a trite poem or baffled by an obscure one.

The experience of satisfied expectation may be what people mean when they speak of "universality" in poetry. They are not talking of some paraphrasable cliché like "love makes the world go 'round" or "war is hell." If it still satisfies our expectations freshly, an "old" poem like William Collins' "Ode" can continue, in spite of changes in fashion and language, to be relevant to contemporary readers.

Poems to read and discuss

SONG FROM MARRIAGE A LA MODE

I

Why should a foolish marriage vow,
  Which long ago was made,
Oblige us to each other now,
  When passion is decayed?
We loved, and we loved, as long as we could,
  'Till our love was loved out in us both;
But our marriage is dead, when the pleasure is fled:
  'Twas pleasure first made it an oath.

II

If I have pleasures for a friend,
  And further love in store,   10
What wrong has he, whose joys did end,
  And who could give no more?
'Tis a madness that he shoud be jealous of me,
  Or that I should bar him of another:
For all we can gain, is to give ourselves pain,
  When neither can hinder the other.

JOHN DRYDEN

A DANCE FOR MILITANT DILETTANTES

No one's going to read
or take you seriously,
a hip friend advises,
until you start coming down on them
like the black poet you truly are
& ink in lots of black in your poems
soul is not enough
you need real color
shining out of real skin
nappy snaggly afro hair   10
baby grow up & dig on *that!*

You got to learn to put in about
stone black fists
coming up against white jaws
& red blood splashing
down those fabled wine & urine-
stained hallways
black bombs blasting out real white estate
the sky itself black with what's to come:
final holocaust   20
the settling up

Dont nobody want no nice nigger no more
these honkies that put out
these books & things
they want an angry splib
a furious nigrah
they dont want no bourgeois woogie
they want them a militant nigger
in a fiji haircut
fresh out of some secret boot camp   30
with a bad book in one hand
& a molotov cocktail in the other
subject to turn up at one of their conferences
or soirees
& shake the shit out of them

NATURALLY

Since Naturally Black is Naturally Beautiful
I must be proud
And, naturally,
Black and
Beautiful
Who always was a trifle
Yellow
And plain though proud
Before.

I've given up pomades   10
Having spent the summer sunning
And feeling naturally free
   (if I die of skin cancer
    oh well—one less
    black and beautiful me)
Yet no Agency spends millions
To prevent my summer tanning
And who trembles nightly
With the fear of their lily cities being swallowed
By a summer ocean of naturally woolly hair?   20

But I've bought my can of
Natural Hair Spray
Made and marketed in Watts
Still thinking more
Proud beautiful black women
Could better make and use
Black bread.

                         AUDRE LORDE

VERNAL SENTIMENT

Though the crocuses poke up their heads in the usual places,
The frog scum appear on the pond with the same froth of
   green,
And boys moon at girls with last year's fatuous faces,
I never am bored, however familiar the scene.

When from under the barn the cat brings a similar litter,—
Two yellow and black, and one that looks in between,—
Though it all happened before, I cannot grow bitter:
I rejoice in the spring, as though no spring ever had been.

THEODORE ROETHKE

CRAZY PIGEON

Crazy pigeon strutting outside my cell—
Go strut on a branch or a steeple bell.
Why coo so softly in this concrete hell?

Fly away, dumb bird. Go winging off free.
Stop coo coo cooing, stop taunting me.
Find your pretty mate and let me be.

Like mine yours might be stone cold in her grave—
And mine too was pretty as a mourning dove.
Dumb prancing pigeon, mourning for your love.

ETHERIDGE KNIGHT

A WINTER SONG

If I
were the
cold weather
and people
talked about me
the way they talk
about it,
I'd just
pack up
and leave town.   10

    WILLIAM J. HARRIS

THE MAN FROM WASHINGTON

The end came easy for most of us.
Packed away in our crude beginnings
in some far corner of a flat world,
we didn't expect much more
than firewood and buffalo robes
to keep us warm. The man came down,
a slouching dwarf with rainwater eyes,
and spoke to us. He promised
that life would go on as usual,
that treaties would be signed, and everyone—   10
man, woman and child—would be innoculated
against a world in which we had no part,
a world of wealth, promise and fabulous disease.

                                JAMES WELCH

CHRISTMAS COMES TO MOCCASIN FLAT

Christmas comes like this: wise men
unhurried, candles bought on credit (poor price
for calves), warriors face down in wine sleep.
Winds cheat to pull heat from smoke.

Friends sit in chinked cabins, stare out
plastic windows and wait for commodities.
Charlie Blackbird, twenty miles from church
and bar, stabs his fire with flint.

When drunks drain radiators for love
or need, chiefs eat snow and talk of change,   10
an urge to laugh pounding their ribs.
Elk play games in high country.

Medicine Woman, clay pipe and twist tobacco,
calls each blizzard by name and predicts
five o'clock by spitting at her television.
Children lean into her breath to beg a story:

Something about honor and passion,
warriors back with meat and song,
a peculiar evening star, quick vision of birth.
Blackbird builds his fire. Outside, a quick thirty below.   20

                                        JAMES WELCH

HOW TO BE UNCLE SAM

My father knew
  how to be
    Uncle Sam.

Six feet two,
  he led the
    parade

the year
  the boys came back
    from war.

Splendidly   10
   spatted, his legs
      like canes,

his dandy coat
   like a
      bluebird's back,

he led the parade,
   and then
      a man

(I've never been sure
   he was honestly   20
      canned—

he might have been
   consciously
      after a laugh)

popped
   from the crowd,
      swinging his hands,

and screamed,
   "You're the s.o.b.
      who takes   30

all my money!"
   and took
      a poke at

my own father.
   He missed
      by half

an inch; he felt
   the wind, my father
      later said.

When the cops   40
   grabbed that one,
      another man

shouted from the
   crowd in a
      voice like brass:

"I don't care if
   you take a poke at
      Updike,

but don't you
   bother   50
      Uncle Sam."

         JOHN UPDIKE

from THE INNER-CITY MOTHER GOOSE

Ding, Dong, Bell

Ding, dong, bell,
The rat control is on the way,
The sweeper trucks are starting to spray,
The garbage trucks are beginning to hum,
The exterminator may even come!

They've got to disinfect it some,
For the mayor's coming to look today
At daily life in a slum.

Fee, Fi, Fo, Fum

Fee, fi, fo, fum,
I smell the blood of violence to come;
I smell the smoke that hangs in the air
Of buildings burning everywhere;
Even the rats abandon the city:
The situation is being studied by a crisis committee.

Wino Will

Wino Will who's drunk his fill
Gets chased by law and order.
Knock him down and kick him around,

That's the way of law and order.
Don't complain or they'll do it again,
Just a law-and-order caper;
Bloody his head and leave him for dead
And keep it out of the paper.

EVE MERRIAM

MANNERS

for a Child of 1918

My grandfather said to me
as we sat on the wagon seat,
"Be sure to remember to always
speak to everyone you meet."

We met a stranger on foot.
My grandfather's whip tapped his hat.
"Good day, sir. Good day. A fine day."
And I said it and bowed where I sat.

Then we overtook a boy we knew
with his big pet crow on his shoulder.   10
"Always offer everyone a ride;
don't forget that when you get older,"

my grandfather said. So Willy
climbed up with us, but the crow
gave a "Caw!" and flew off. I was worried.
How would he know where to go?

But he flew a little way at a time
from fence post to fence post, ahead;
and when Willy whistled he answered.
"A fine bird," my grandfather said,   20

"and he's well brought up. See, he answers
nicely when he's spoken to.
Man or beast, that's good manners.
Be sure that you both always do."

When automobiles went by,
the dust hid the people's faces,
but we shouted "Good day! Good day!
Fine day!" at the top of our voices.

When we came to Hustler Hill,
he said that the mare was tired,   30
so we all got down and walked,
as our good manners required.

ELIZABETH BISHOP

WASH.   RINSE.   DRY.

there is a negro lying on his side
in the back seat of your station wagon
knees drawn up   (he is a tall negro)   feet
in heavy work shoes stuck out in the air
(he is thoughtful)   there's a rag in his hand

he was the last in the line of workers
spraying   scrubbing   rinsing   some dressed up in
yellow slickers like sea-captains   this man's
particular job is to jump in back
seats and clean the rear windows   (the last touch)   10

you were supposed to wait till it was done
dry and sparkling   let him out   leave a tip
in the box   pay the cashier   and drive off.
understandably in a hurry you
got the rest done but forgot about him

now you're trying to get home in time for
supper   he's relaxed and very polite
not saying a word   you could drive him back
to the garage or let him off near his
house   or just let him stay in your back seat   20
maybe he would like to sit back there and
look after things and keep your windows clean

DICK LOURIE

REBELS FROM FAIRY TALES

We are the frogs who will not turn to princes.
We will not change our green and slippery skin
for one so lily-pale and plain, so smooth
it seems to have no grain. We will not leave
our leap, our spring, accordion. We have
seen ourselves in puddles, and we like
our grin. Men are so up and down, so thin
they look like walking trees. Their knees seem stiff,
and we have seen men shooting hares and deer.
They're queer . . . they even war with one another!   10
They've stretched too far from earth and natural things
for us to admire. We prefer to lie
close to the water looking at the sky
reflected; contemplating how the sun,
Great Rana, can thrust his yellow, webbed foot
through all the elements in a giant jump;
can poke the bottom of the brook; warm
the stumps for us to sit upon; and heat
our backs. Men have forgotten to relax.
They bring their noisy boxes, and the blare   20
insults the air. We cannot hear the cheer
of crickets, nor our own dear booming chugs.
Frogs wouldn't even eat men's legs.
We scorn their warm, dry princesses. We're proud
of our own bug-eyed brides with bouncing strides.
Keep your magic. We are not such fools.
Here is the ball without a claim on it.
We may begin from the same tadpoles, but
we've thought a bit, and will not turn to men.

                                        HYACINTHE HILL

FOR A LAMB

I saw on the slant hill a putrid lamb,
Propped with daisies. The sleep looked deep,
The face nudged in the green pillow
But the guts were out for crows to eat.

Where's the lamb? whose tender plaint
Said all for the mute breezes.
Say he's in the wind somewhere,
Say, there's a lamb in the daisies.

RICHARD EBERHART

POLITICS

"In our time the destiny of man presents its meaning in
political terms." THOMAS MANN

How can I, that girl standing there,
My attention fix
On Roman or on Russian
Or on Spanish politics?
Yet here's a travelled man that knows
What he talks about,
And there's a politician
That has read and thought,
And maybe what they say is true
Of war and war's alarms,   10
But O that I were young again
And held her in my arms!

WILLIAM BUTLER YEATS

ON THE DEATH OF A FAVOURITE CAT

Drowned in a Tub of Gold-fishes

'Twas on a lofty vase's side,
Where China's gayest art had dy'd
The azure flowers, that blow;
Demurest of the tabby kind,
The pensive Selima reclin'd,
Gazed on the lake below.

Her conscious tail her joy declar'd;
The fair round face, the snowy beard,
The velvet of her paws,

Her coat, that with the tortoise vies,   10
Her ears of jet, and emerald eyes,
She saw; and purr'd applause.

Still had she gazed; but 'midst the tide
Two angel forms were seen to glide,
The Genii of the stream:
Their scaly armour's Tyrian hue
Thro' richest purple to the view
Betray'd a golden gleam.

The hapless nymph with wonder saw:
A whisker first, and then a claw,   20
With many an ardent wish,
She stretch'd in vain to reach the prize:—
What female heart can gold despise?
What Cat's averse to fish?

Presumptuous maid! with looks intent
Again she stretch'd, again she bent,
Nor knew the gulf between.
(Malignant fate sat by, and smiled)
The slippery verge her feet beguiled,
She tumbled headlong in.   30

Eight times emerging from the flood
She mew'd to ev'ry watery God,
Some speedy aid to send.
No Dolphin came, no Nereid stirr'd:
Nor cruel Tom, nor Susan heard.
A favourite has no friend!

From hence, ye beauties undeceived,
Know, one false step is ne'er retrieved,
And be with caution bold.
Not all that tempts your wandering eyes   40
And heedless hearts, is lawful prize:
Nor all, that glisters, gold.

                    THOMAS GRAY

7
What Finally Matters

Although we have emphasized how sounds, rhythms, details, and shapes contribute to the content of individual poems, we have not talked about these elements as ends in themselves. We value them only because they lead us into the meaning of the poems. What finally matters is the way each individual experiences poetry.

No one can tell you the experiences to have or how to have them. Moreover, much of what happens in a poem, as in all of life, occurs without your choice and you're stuck with it. Obviously, the things that happen to you can be painful as well as pleasant. If you look back over your notebook you will probably find a record showing both enjoyment and dislike in your responses to the poems you have read. If you look back at the poems themselves you will find that some seem remote and uninteresting, others familiar and immediate.

Because we believe that a reader's individual response is what finally counts in poetry, we want to end this book with three poems we like very much. Since expectations and interests differ, no one can honestly enjoy every poem he reads. But for us, these three poems successfully bridge the gap between the poets' experiences and our own.

MY WICKED UNCLE

It was my first funeral.
Some loss of status as a nephew since
Dictates that I recall
My numbness, my grandfather's hesitance,
My five aunts busy in the hall.

I found him closeted with living souls—
Coffined to perfection in the bedroom.
Death had deprived him of his mustache,
His thick horn-rimmed spectacles,
The easy corners of his salesman dash   10
(Those things by which I had remembered him)
And sundered him behind unnatural gauze.
His hair was badly parted on the right
As if for Sunday school. That night
I saw my uncle as he really was.

The narrative he dispensed was mostly
Wicked avuncular fantasy—
He went in for waistcoats and haircream.
But something about him
Demanded that you picture the surprise   20
Of the chairman of the board, when to
'What will you have with your whiskey?' my uncle replies—
'Another whiskey, please.'

Once he was jailed in New York
Twice on the same day—
The crookedest chief steward in the Head Line.
And once (he affected communism)
He brought the whole crew out on strike
In protest at the loss of a day's pay
Crossing the international date line.   30

They buried him slowly above the sea,
The young Presbyterian minister
Rumpled and windy in the sea air.
A most absorbing ceremony—
Ashes to ashes, dust to dust.
I saw sheep huddled in the long wet grass
Of the golf-course, and the empty freighters
Sailing for ever down Belfast Lough

In a fine rain, their sirens going,
As the gradual graph of my uncle's life and   40
Times dipped precipitately
Into the bowels of Carnmoney Cemetery.

His teenage kids are growing horns and claws—
More wicked already than ever my uncle was.

DEREK MAHON

LONESOME IN THE COUNTRY

How much of me is sandwiches radio beer?
How much pizza traffic & neon messages?
I take thoughtful journeys to supermarkets,
philosophize about the newest good movie,
camp out at magazine racks & on floors,
catch humanity leering back in laundromats,
invent shortcuts by the quarter hour

There's meaning to all this itemization
& I'd do well to look for it in woodpiles
or in hills & springs or trees in the woods   10
instead of staying in the shack all the time
imagining too much
                    falling asleep in old chairs

All that childhood I spent in farmhouses
& still cant tell one bush from another—
Straight wilderness would wipe me out
faster than cancer from cigarette smoke

Meantime my friends are out all day long
stomping thru the woods all big-eyed
& that's me walking the road afternoons
head in a book
                    all that hilly sweetness wasting   20

                              AL YOUNG

SPITTING ON IRA ROSENBLATT

It was a great pleasure
spitting on Ira Rosenblatt
a fine forbidden thing
denied me by his mother
and my mother to ensure
that I would pass my Sundays
spitting on Ira Rosenblatt

He in the alley, I on the wall
spitting on Ira Rosenblatt's
hair and face and shoulders   10

204   WHAT FINALLY MATTERS

each time he tried to escape
It was a fine thing to torment him
such a sweet and industrious pleasure
spitting on Ira Rosenblatt

Working up the spittle, a duty:
spitting on Ira Rosenblatt
I spit in the toilet these days
There is no one left to torment that way
not that willing and straightforward way
How pleasant Sundays were, high on a wall   20
spitting on Ira Rosenblatt

ROBERT HERSHON

Imagine you were ending this book: what three poems would you
choose?

Appendix

HOW TO WRITE ABOUT POETRY

Writing about poetry is very much like writing about any other subject. Whatever your subject, whether it is a poem or a public issue, you express your response to it as well as give facts about it. But it isn't enough to decide how you feel about a work, then repeat over and over in your paper "I like it" or "I don't like it." The first question someone else reading your paper will ask is "Why?"

Instead of waiting for someone else to ask the question, ask it yourself. How does the poem make its impression on you? Are you responding mostly to what the poem says (perhaps you and the poet have similar interests or experiences) or to the techniques the poet uses to get his subject across? Or are you responding to a combination of both? You might find that a poem you would expect to like because of its subject matter leaves you cold because it is jingly or vague. Other poems may, through their use of sounds or details or other poetic tools, interest you in something you never cared about before.

While you are considering your own reactions to the poem, you should also try to decide how the poet wants you to respond. What words, sounds, or rhythms does the poet use to share his experiences or to convince you to see things the way he does? How has he arranged these technical elements to affect you, the reader? What purposes might he have had in mind when writing? How does he let you know his purpose through the poem?

Every paper, no matter what the subject is, needs to make some point. You've probably already found yourself objecting to some poems as "pointless," and a pointless paper is at least as bad as a pointless poem. A "point," however, doesn't have to be (though it easily may be) more unusual than an honest statement of like or dislike. What *is* pointless is a paper that "ana-

206

lyzes" a poem without any apparent cause or conclusion. When trying to think of the "point" of your paper, ask yourself why someone else reading it might be interested. What can another person reading your paper gain from it? You can always at least show him a point of view other than his own.

After deciding on the point you want to make, which often happens after you've done most of your thinking, it is a good idea to place your statement of purpose somewhere close to the beginning of your paper. This becomes your general idea or theme. The rest of your paper is then a matter of working out this general idea. The facts and ideas you include should be chosen to support or illustrate the theme. Most of the relevant facts for your paper are in the poem itself and are a mix of the contents and techniques present in the work. Your consideration of the "facts" and ideas of the poem is the place for "analysis." Remember, it is not necessary to cover everything about a poem in your paper. You need only that which will support your theme. Your conclusion wraps up your theme and drives home your point.

You probably already have a good idea of how to write about a poem. But, if you just cannot get going—and starting can be the hardest part—try writing freely about the poem. To do this, read the poem several times to yourself until you feel you understand it, and then, putting the poem aside, write *without stopping* until you've run through your reactions. Don't worry if what you write doesn't always seem relevant to the poem or isn't always in proper English. The important things are that you are making a start, loosening up, and also recording some honest, impromptu reactions to the poem, not false and pretentious ones. If the free writing exercise doesn't work the first time, try again at a moment you feel more in the mood for it. You can then take the results of your free writing, keep what you like (don't be afraid to leave unwanted words and ideas behind), and make a fresh start on your paper, organizing it as described in the preceding paragraph.

For an example of this general approach to writing about poetry, let's look at Denise Levertov's poem "The Secret," which appears on pages 15 and 16 at the end of Chapter 1, and imagine one possible paper we might write about it.

"THE SECRET" BY DENISE LEVERTOV

Secrets are the stuff of adventure stories. Can they also be the stuff of poetry? In dealing with this question Denise Levertov's "Secret" tells us something about poetry as well as about people.

Adventure stories keep their secrets until the end. Our curiosity is aroused and the story's suspense is kept up until the secret is told. Denise Levertov turns this formula upside down. Our expectations are unsettled. She tells us the secret in her second line and then almost immediately takes it back. Two girls had discovered "the secret of life" in a line from one of her poems, but they never told her what it was, and not knowing "the secret" herself, the poet couldn't guess what it might be the girls had found. At this point we are forced to ask ourselves, Is there really a secret of life? Is the poem really about that secret?

A good adventure story plants clues that lead to the solution of the mystery at the end. A good poem does the same. One of the first things we notice about "The Secret" is its shape, the way it is put together. The poem is written in stanzas of four short lines each, without rhymes, and punctuated like prose; sentences are sometimes complete within one stanza and at other times run from stanza to stanza. Throughout the poem, too, the sentences get longer and longer. Beginning with two short, matter-of-fact ones, followed by two longer, more qualified ones, the poem reaches its climax in the long, run-on sentence beginning "I love them / for finding what / I can't find." This climactic sentence suggests a rush of uncontrollable feeling. The poem then concludes with a relatively short sentence stating what Levertov values most of all—the girls' belief that there is a secret of life.

When we read "The Secret" aloud we find the rhythms parallel the poem's shape. The first stanza is crisp, precise, perfectly suited to its matter-of-fact statement. The second stanza introduces a slower, more hesitant quality into the voice. This hesitant, uncertain note is maintained until line 18 with the assertion "I love them." At this point the rhythm picks up in tempo, leaping across pauses demanded by the ends of lines, commas, and stanza breaks until it reaches line 30 in the word "happenings." The cumulative effect of the rhythm is to reinforce the emotional quality suggested by the grammatical structure of the sentence. Beginning with the linking word "And" the rhythm slows down again gradually, but remains strong and suggests a thoughtful, reflective mood.

While there are no details that appeal to the senses in this poem, unlike other poems by Denise Levertov (see pages 83 and 126), the poet is very careful to tell us exactly who discovered the secret, what the secret was called by the girls who discovered it, what the poet's reactions were to learning about the discovery, that a third person who knew no more than that the discovery was "the secret of life" told her about it, and that the poet herself didn't know the secret. These nonsensory and abstract details are appropriate to a subject that is mainly concerned with ideas.

The reader's attention is directed to the central idea of the poem, and he learns gradually that "the secret of life" cannot be fixed once and for all but instead appears many times in many places with many forms. It cannot be named any more precisely than it has been because it is extremely private. Even the person who has given the secret to someone else cannot be sure of what it is or if there is such a secret. All that she can be sure of is that it was exhilarating to have given it, whatever it was, to another person.

The poem has another "secret" also. This secret is about how poetry works. Here we have a poem written in response to a poet's learning what a reader's response was to an earlier poem. Levertov suggests that although poetry may not be a perfect medium for the communication of facts it can generate emotional states that have a validity of their own beyond the realm of mere fact. This secret, as she says, remains to be discovered again and again.

Index

American Indian, Traditional "Twelfth Song of the Thunder" 42; "The Whole World Is Coming" 179; "A Woman's Complaint" 106

Atwood, Margaret "Dreams of the Animals" 152; "Game After Supper" 108

Auden, W. H. "Miss Gee" 168; "Who's Who" 61

Ballads by Unknown Authors "Bonnie George Campbell" 136; "Jesse James" 137; "Lydia Sherman Is Plagued with Rats" 167

Barks, Coleman "Appendix" 92; "Big Toe" 92; "Bruises" 92; "Cavities" 93; "Goosepimples" 93

Bishop, Elizabeth "Manners" 195; "Sestina" 165

Black, D. M. "The Educators" 148

Blake, William "London" 46; "Nurse's Song," from *Songs of Innocence* 72; "Nurse's Song," from *Songs of Experience* 72

Bly, Robert "Sleet Storm on the Merritt Parkway" 28

Brooks, Gwendolyn "The Ballad of Rudolph Reed" 155; "The Empty Woman" 31; "a song in the front yard" 10; "We Real Cool" 30

Clifton, Lucille "The 1st" 11

Coleridge, Samuel Taylor "Kubla Khan" 47

Collins, William "Ode Written in the Beginning of the Year 1746" 184

Crapsey, Adelaide "November Night" 24; "Triad" 68

Cruz, Victor Hernandez "going uptown to visit miriam" 73

cummings, e. e. "Buffalo Bill's Defunct" 171

Daniel, Samuel "Sonnet 45" 150

Dickinson, Emily "Because I Could Not Stop for Death" 33; "I Heard a Fly Buzz— When I Died" 38

Dryden, John "A Song for Saint Cecilia's Day, 1687" 43; "Song," from *Marraige a la Mode* 187

Duff, Gerald "The Deep Breather" 77

Dunagan, Randy "Senior citizens' city" 87

Dunbar, Paul Lawrence "We Wear the Mask" 161

Durem, Ray "Award" 47

Earley, Jaci "One Thousand Nine Hundred & Sixty-Eight Winters" 100

Eberhart, Richard "For a Lamb" 198

Eckman, Margaret "He Returned from the Mine" 121

Eliot, T. S. "Aunt Helen" 143; "Morning at the Window" 89; "The Waste Land" 180

Field, Edward "Unwanted" 162

Fisher, Roy "The Hospital in Winter" 163

Fraser, Kathleen "Poem in Which My Legs Are Accepted" 104

Freeman, Carol "Christmas morning i" 97

Frost, Robert "The Fear" 157; "Out, Out—" 36

George, Phil "Ambition" 77

Giovanni, Nikki "Alabama Poem" 130; "For Saundra" 20; "Master Charge Blues" 150

Goldsmith, Oliver "Song" 179

Goncalves, Joe "Now the Time Is Ripe to Be" 129

Gray, Thomas "Elegy in a Country Churchyard" 26; "On the Death of a Favourite Cat" 199

Hall, Donald "The Man in the Dead Machine" 101

Hardy, Thomas "During Wind and Rain" 45

Harper, Michael S. "We Assume" 166

Harris, William J. "My Friend, Wendell Berry" 167; "Samantha Is My Negro Cat" 114; "A Winter Song" 190
Hayden, Robert "Idol" 29; "Market" 85; "Runagate Runagate" 78; "Snow" 185; "The Whipping" 7
Henderson, David "Number 5—December" 102
Herbert, George "Easter Wings" 128
Herrick, Robert "Delight in Disorder" 66
Hershon, Robert "Spitting on Ira Rosenblatt" 204
Hill, Hyacinthe "Rebels from Fairy Tales" 198
Housman, A. E. "To an Athlete Dying Young" 64
Hughes, Langston "Ballad of the Landlord" 4; "Could Be" 137

Jones, LeRoi "For Hettie" 183; "Preface to a Twenty Volume Suicide Note" 70

Keats, John "A Fragment" 17; "On the Grasshopper and Cricket" 139
Knight, Etheridge "Crazy Pigeon" 170; "For Black Poets Who Think of Suicide" 18
Knoepfle, John "October scrimmage" 38

Lachs, John "Father" 76; "Houses" 91
Landor, Walter Savage "On His Seventy-fifth Birthday" 181
Lawson, David "No Great Matter" 177
Lear, Edward "The Owl and the Pussy-Cat" 173
Lee, Don L. "Big Momma" 134; "But He Was Cool or; he even stopped for green lights" 75; "Mixed Sketches" 94
Lester, Julius "Parents" 122; "The War—II" 123

Levertov, Denise "A Day Begins" 83; "Merritt Parkway" 126; "The Secret" 15
Lindsay, Vachel "The Flower-Fed Buffaloes" 6
Lorde, Audre "Naturally" 189
Lourie, Dick "Wash. Rinse. Dry." 196
Lucie-Smith, Edward "Silence" 39

Mahon, Derek "My Wicked Uncle" 202
Major, Clarence "The Doll Believers" 108
Masters, Edgar Lee "Harry Wilmans" 103
McCarthy, Eugene "Bicycle Rider (to Mary)" 91; "Saturday" 90
McConnel, Frances "Here I am . . ." 18; "Highway 5 Toward Vancouver" 116
Melville, Herman "Shiloh." 29
Merriam, Eve "Ding, Dong, Bell" 194; "Fee, Fi, Fo, Fum" 194; "I Had a Little Teevee" 180; "Wino Will" 194
Millay, Edna St. Vincent "Sonnet 16" 140
Milton, John "Sonnet 12" 160
Moore, Judith "For A High-School Commencement" 151
Moore, Merrill "How She Resolved to Act" 62; "Old men and old women going home on the street car" 141
Morris, John N. "The Dream in the City" 60

Olson, Ted "Mending a Sidewalk . . . Making a Poem" 12
Owen, Wilfred "Anthem for Doomed Youth" 184; "Arms and the Boy" 49; "Disabled" 117

Parker, Patricia "Assassination" 59; "Sometimes My Husband" 99

Patchen, Kenneth "The Birds Are Very Careful of This World" 147; "He's Either Going Away or Coming Back" 147; "I Have a Funny Feeling" 146; "Pleasantly We Shall Remain" 146
Patterson, Ray "You Are the Brave" 49
Phillips, Frank Lamont "When It Was Cold" 115
Piercy, Marge "The Consumer" 44; "The Crippling" 102; "morning half-life blues" 111
Poole, Tom "I Wonder Why" 84
Pope, Alexander "Epistle to Miss Blount, on Her Leaving the Town, After the Coronation" 109

Raffel, Burton "On Watching the Construction of a Skyscraper" 24
Reed, Ishmael "Beware: Do Not Read This Poem" 1
Roethke, Theodore "Dolor" 93; "My Papa's Waltz" 52; "Night Journey" 69; "Vernal Sentiment" 189
Rutsala, Vern "Listening" 37; "Other Lives" 97
Ryan, Therl "Autumn Woman" 133

Seay, James "Options" 119
Shakespeare, William "Sonnet 55" 14; "Sonnet 73" 139; "Sonnet 130" 117
Shelley, Percy Bysshe "The Indian Serenade" 182
Shirley, James "Death the Leveller" 161
Simpson, Louis "American Poetry" 18; "Carentan O Carentan" 153
Snyder, Gary "Hay for the Horses" 5
Spenser, Edmund "Prothalamion" 52
Spriggs, Edward S. "For the TRUTH (because it is necessary)" 76

Swift, Jonathan "A Beautiful Young Nymph Going to Bed" 106; "A Description of the Morning" 88; "A Satirical Elegy on the Death of a Late Famous General" 71

Tate, James "Flight" 25; "Stray Animals" 110
Tennyson, Alfred, Lord "The Sleeping Beauty" 176
Thomas, Dylan "Do Not Go Gentle into That Good Night" 145; "The Hunchback in the Park" 112
Thomas, Richard W. "The Worker" 21

Updike, John "How to Be Uncle Sam" 192; "The

Menagerie at Versailles in 1775" 148; "Sonic Boom" 39

Van Dias, Robert "Dump Poem" 14

Walsh, Chad "Port Authority Terminal: 9 a.m. Monday" 131
Watson, Patricia "Lament for a Brother" 58
Welch, James "Christmas Comes to Moccasin Flat" 192; "The Man from Washington" 191
Whitewing, Donna "August 24, 1963—1:00 A.M.— Omaha" 69
Whitman, Walt "A Noiseless Patient Spider" 41; from "Song of Myself" 11;

"When I Heard the Learn'd Astronomer" 35
Willard, Nancy "The Graffiti Poet" 16
Williams, William Carlos "Poem" 126; "Smell!" 142; "Young Woman at a Window" 96
Wordsworth, William "My Heart Leaps Up" 181; "Sonnet Composed upon Westminster Bridge" 67; "The World Is Too Much with Us" 60

Yeats, William Butler "Politics" 199
Young, Al "Birthday Poem" 164; "The Curative Powers of Silence" 40; "A Dance for Militant Dilletantes" 188; "Lonesome in the Country" 204

(credits and acknowledgments continued.)

RICHARD EBERHART. "For a Lamb" is from COLLECTED POEMS 1930-1960 by Richard Eberhart. Copyright © 1960 by Richard Eberhart. Reprinted by permission of Oxford University Press, Inc., Chatto & Windus, Ltd. and Richard Eberhart.
MARGARET ECKMAN. "he returned from the mine . . ." is reprinted by permission of The World Publishing Company from STUFF by Herbert Kohl and Victor Hernandez Cruz. Copyright © 1970 by Herbert Kohl and Victor Hernandez Cruz. Reprinted by permission of the Robert Lescher Literary Agency.
T. S. ELIOT. "Morning at the Window," "Aunt Helen," and lines 253-56 from "The Waste Land" are from COLLECTED POEMS 1909-1962 by T. S. Eliot, copyright 1936 by Harcourt Brace Jovanovich, Inc., copyright © 1963, 1964 by T. S. Eliot. Reprinted by permission of the publishers.
EDWARD FIELD. "Unwanted" is reprinted from STAND UP, FRIEND, WITH ME by Edward Field by permission of Grove Press, Inc. Copyright © 1963 by Edward Field.
ROY FISHER. "The Hospital in Winter" copyright © Roy Fisher, from COLLECTED POEMS, Fulcrum Press, London, 1969. Reprinted by permission of Fulcrum Press.
KATHLEEN FRASER. "Poem in Which My Legs Are Accepted" is reprinted by permission of the author.
CAROL FREEMAN. "Christmas morning i," copyright © 1968 by Carol Freeman, is reprinted from BLACK FIRE, edited by LeRoi Jones and Larry Neal, William Morrow & Company. Used with permission of the author and the Ronald Hobbs Literary Agency.
ROBERT FROST. "The Fear" is reprinted from THE POETRY OF ROBERT FROST edited by Edward Connery Lathem. Copyright 1930, 1939, © 1969 by Holt, Rinehart & Winston, Inc. Copyright © 1958 by Robert Frost. Copyright © 1967 by Lesley Frost Ballantine. Reprinted by permission of Holt, Rinehart & Winston, Inc. "Out, Out—" is reprinted from THE POETRY OF ROBERT FROST. Copyright 1916, © 1969 by Holt, Rinehart & Winston, Inc. Copyright 1944 by Robert Frost. Reprinted by permission of Holt, Rinehart & Winston, Inc.
PHIL GEORGE. "Ambition" is reprinted from South Dakota Review.
NIKKI GIOVANNI. "For Saundra" is reprinted from BLACK JUDGMENT by Nikki Giovanni, © 1969 by Nikki Giovanni and published by Broadside Press. "Alabama Poem" and "Master Charge Blues" are reprinted from RE:CREATION by Nikki Giovanni, © 1970 by Nikki Giovanni and published by Broadside Press.
JOE GONCALVES. "Now the Time Is Ripe to Be" copyright © 1968 by Joe Goncalves, is reprinted from BLACK FIRE edited by LeRoi Jones and Larry Neal, William Morrow & Company. Used with permission of the author and the Ronald Hobbs Literary Agency.
DONALD HALL. "The Man in the Dead Machine" is reprinted from THE ALLIGATOR BRIDE: POEMS NEW AND SELECTED by Donald Hall. Copyright © 1966 by Donald Hall. By permission of Harper & Row Publishers, Inc.

212

PHOTO CREDITS